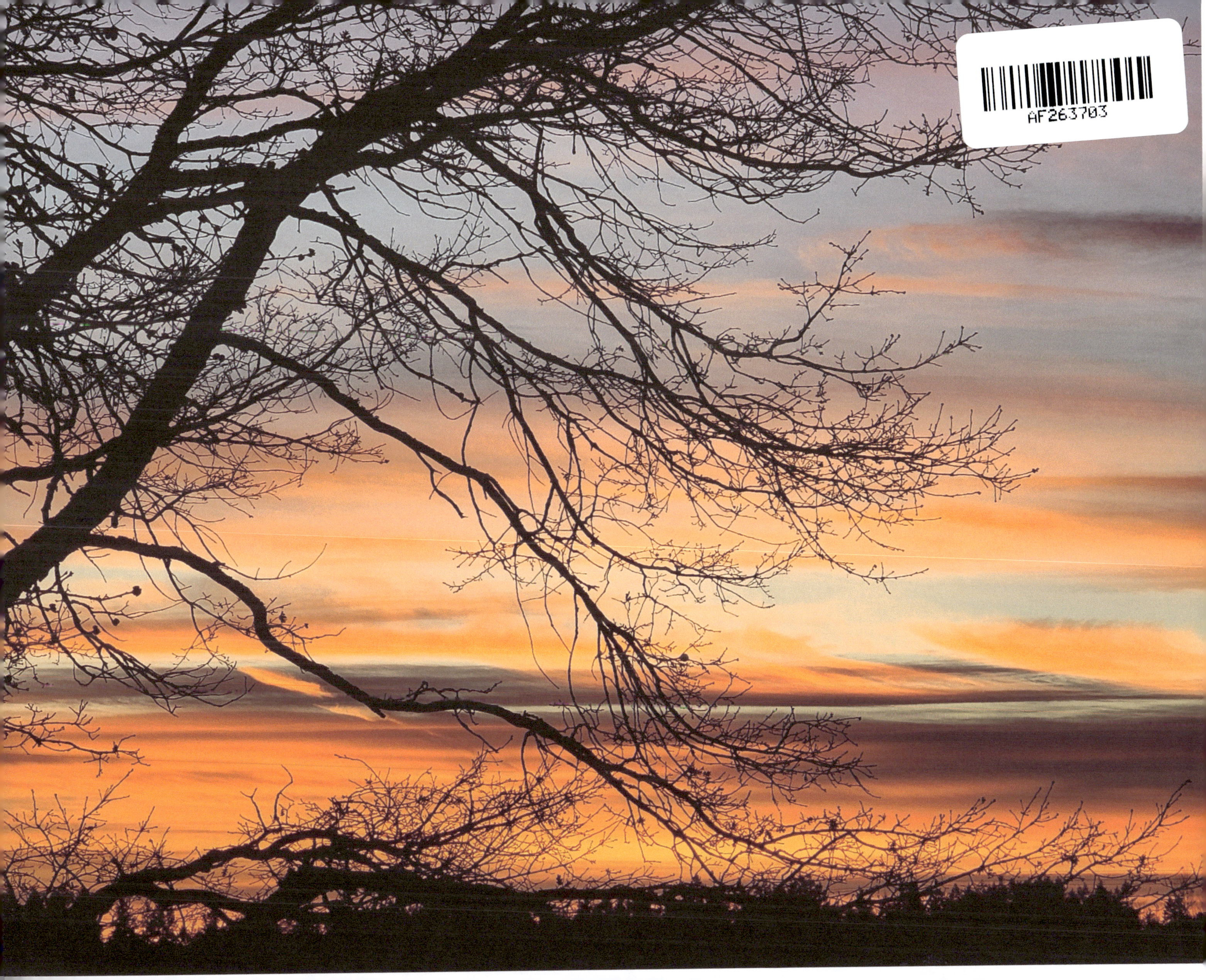

AF263703

PUBLISHED BY ARLEDGE COMICS, LLC

Jordaan Arledge, founder & publisher

Sharron Arledge, cofounder & v.p. of creative development

Zach Sherwood, director of operations

Natalie Cooper, senior editor

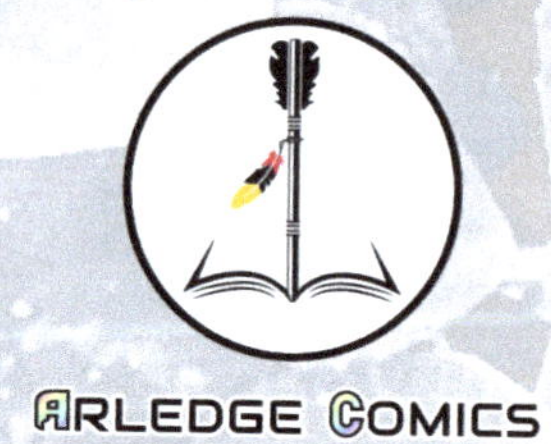

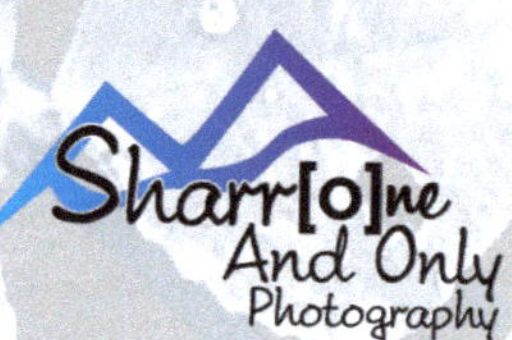

ARLEDGECOMICS.COM
LINKTR.EE/ARLEDGECOMICS

First Printing, Fall 2024

ISBN: 978-1-949898-15-6

1 2 3 4 5 6 7 8 9 10

Printed in the USA

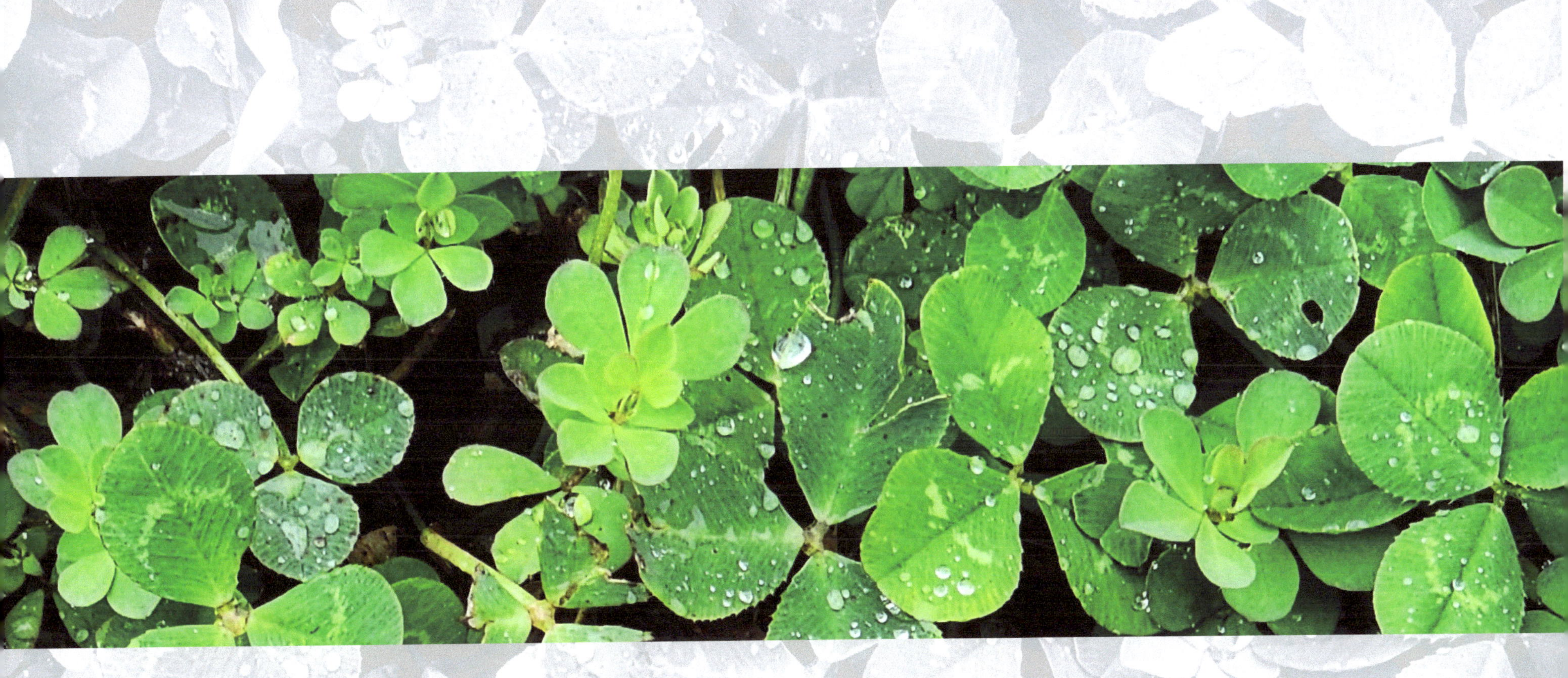

Shuttered Stanzas

Photography by Sharron Arledge

Written by Jordaan Arledge

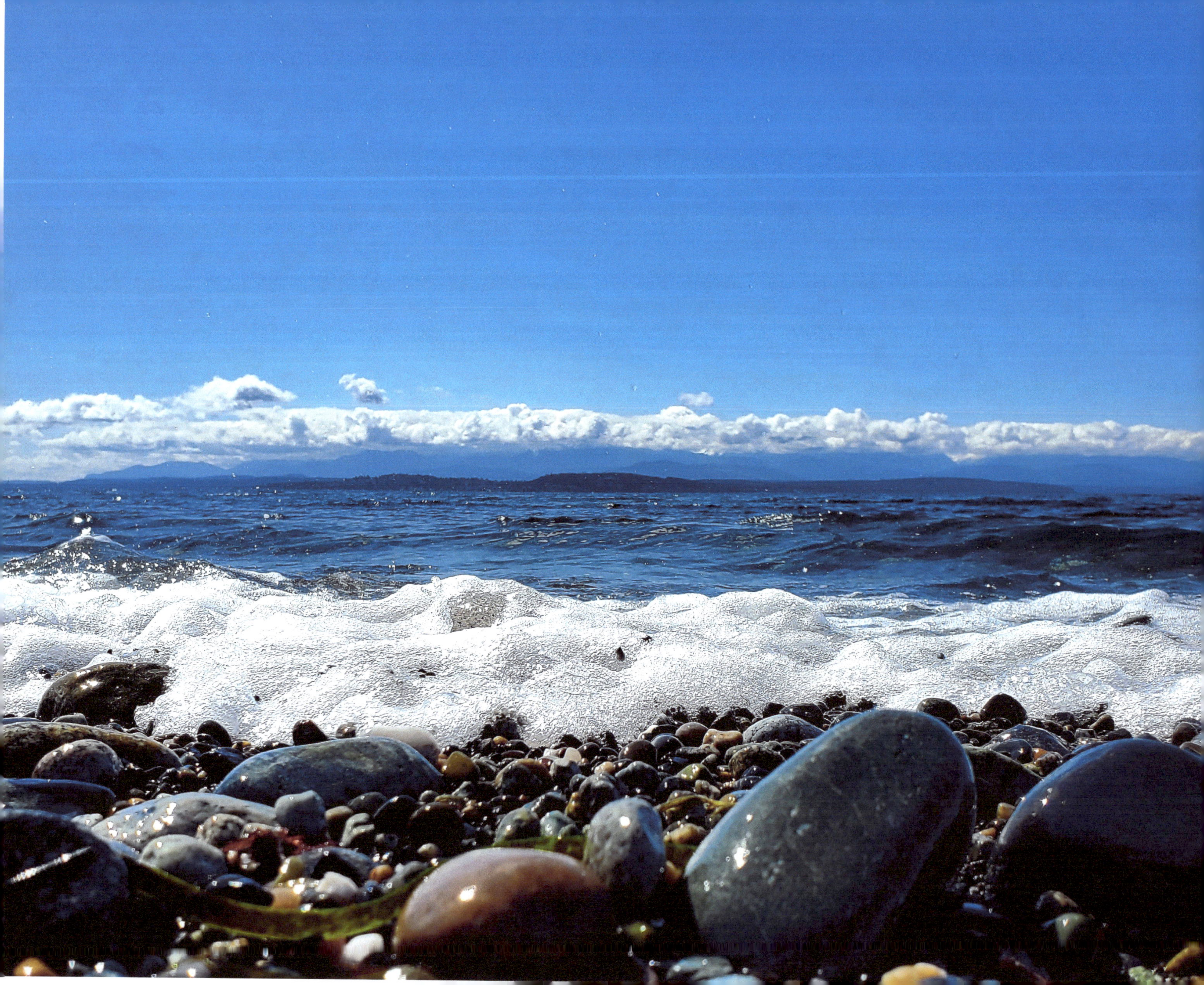

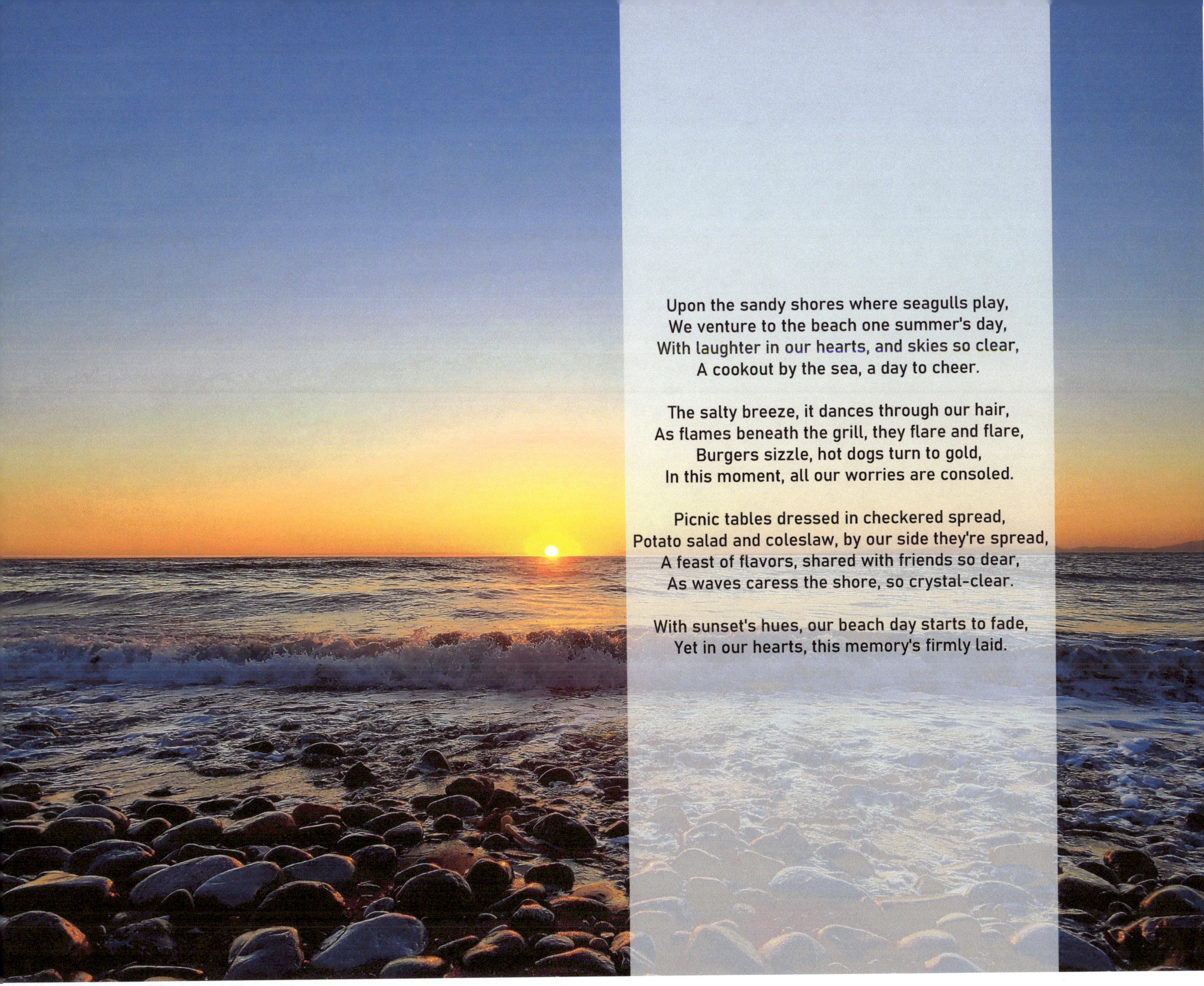

Upon the sandy shores where seagulls play,
We venture to the beach one summer's day,
With laughter in our hearts, and skies so clear,
A cookout by the sea, a day to cheer.

The salty breeze, it dances through our hair,
As flames beneath the grill, they flare and flare,
Burgers sizzle, hot dogs turn to gold,
In this moment, all our worries are consoled.

Picnic tables dressed in checkered spread,
Potato salad and coleslaw, by our side they're spread,
A feast of flavors, shared with friends so dear,
As waves caress the shore, so crystal-clear.

With sunset's hues, our beach day starts to fade,
Yet in our hearts, this memory's firmly laid.

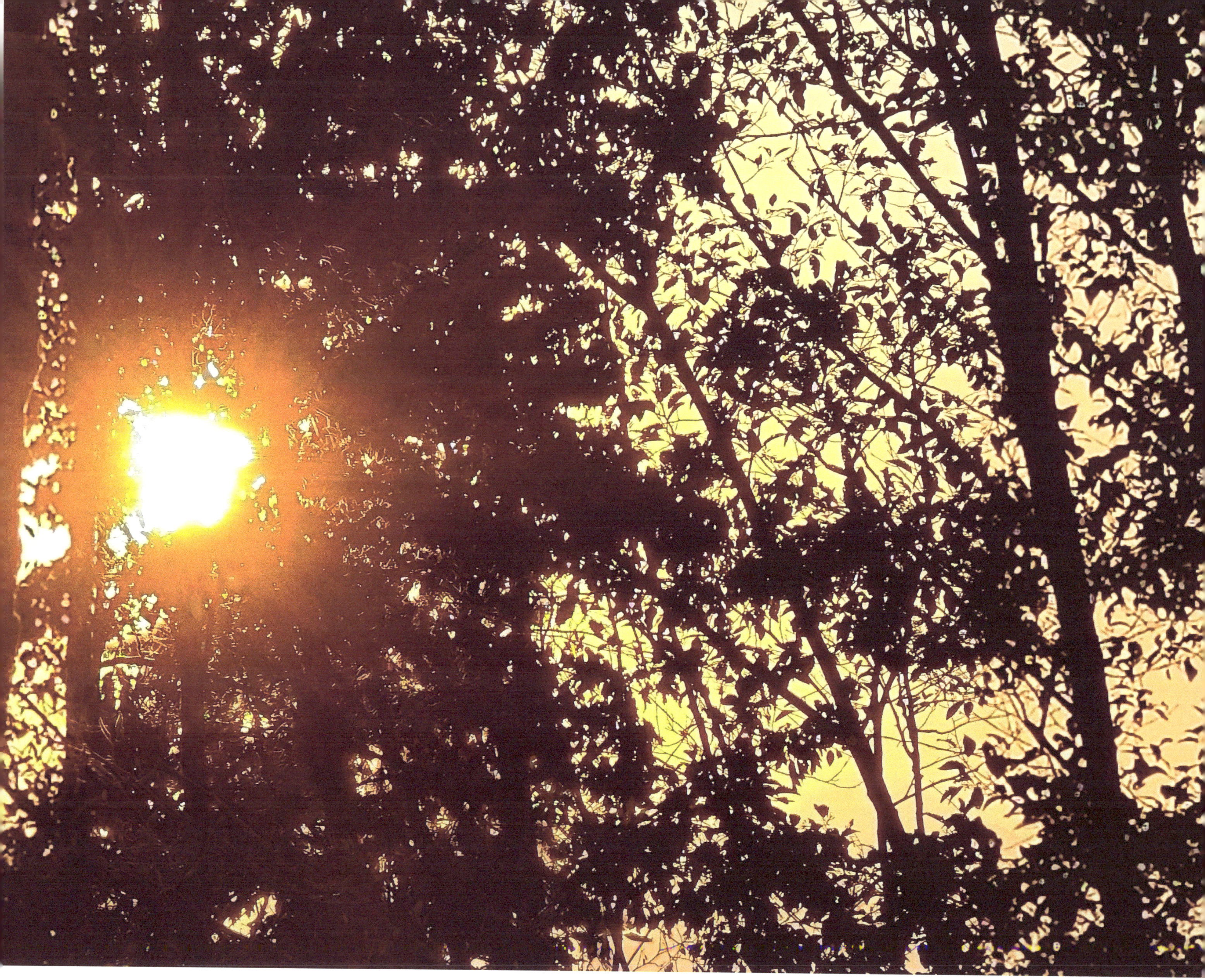

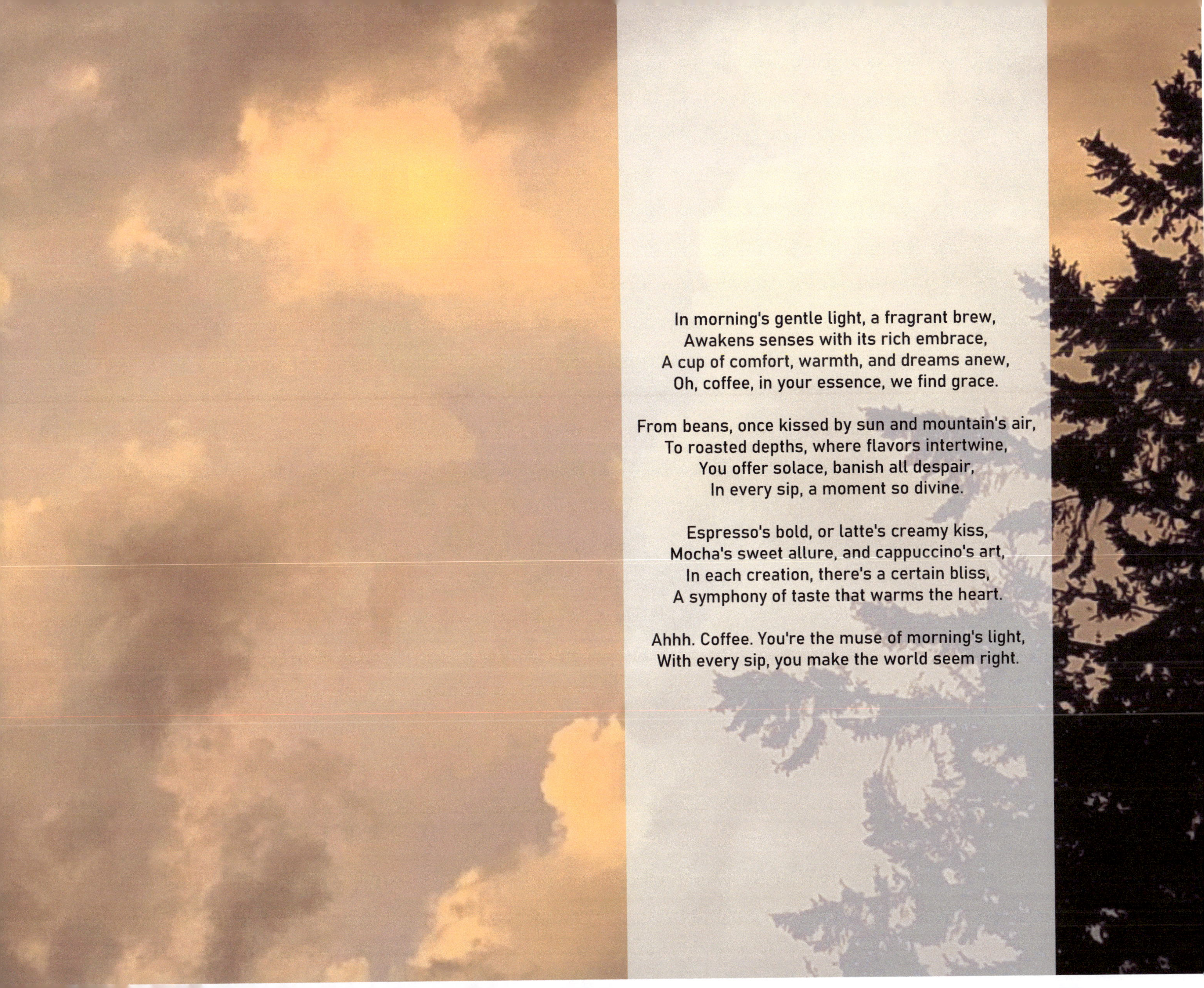

In morning's gentle light, a fragrant brew,
Awakens senses with its rich embrace,
A cup of comfort, warmth, and dreams anew,
Oh, coffee, in your essence, we find grace.

From beans, once kissed by sun and mountain's air,
To roasted depths, where flavors intertwine,
You offer solace, banish all despair,
In every sip, a moment so divine.

Espresso's bold, or latte's creamy kiss,
Mocha's sweet allure, and cappuccino's art,
In each creation, there's a certain bliss,
A symphony of taste that warms the heart.

Ahhh. Coffee. You're the muse of morning's light,
With every sip, you make the world seem right.

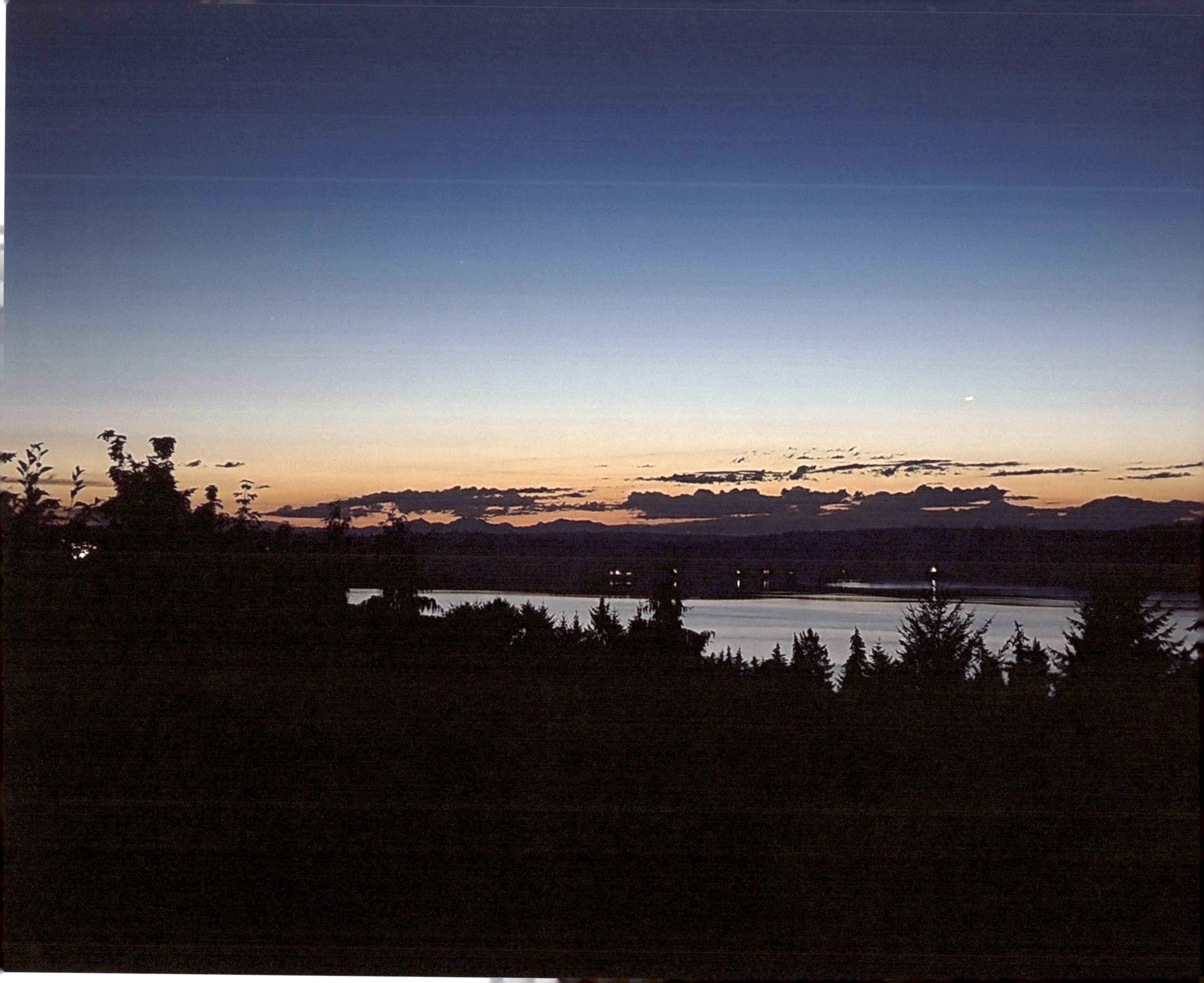

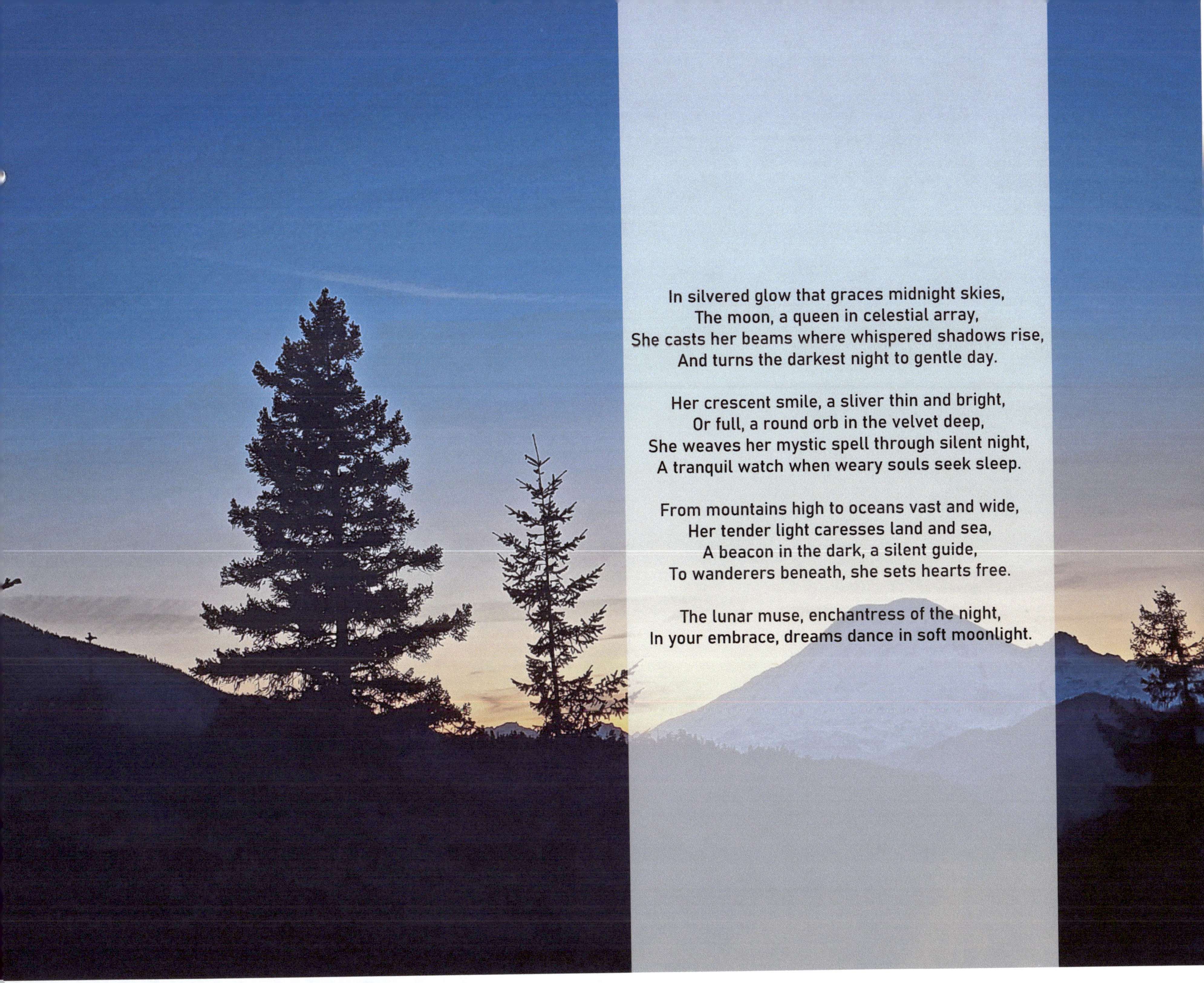

In silvered glow that graces midnight skies,
The moon, a queen in celestial array,
She casts her beams where whispered shadows rise,
And turns the darkest night to gentle day.

Her crescent smile, a sliver thin and bright,
Or full, a round orb in the velvet deep,
She weaves her mystic spell through silent night,
A tranquil watch when weary souls seek sleep.

From mountains high to oceans vast and wide,
Her tender light caresses land and sea,
A beacon in the dark, a silent guide,
To wanderers beneath, she sets hearts free.

The lunar muse, enchantress of the night,
In your embrace, dreams dance in soft moonlight.

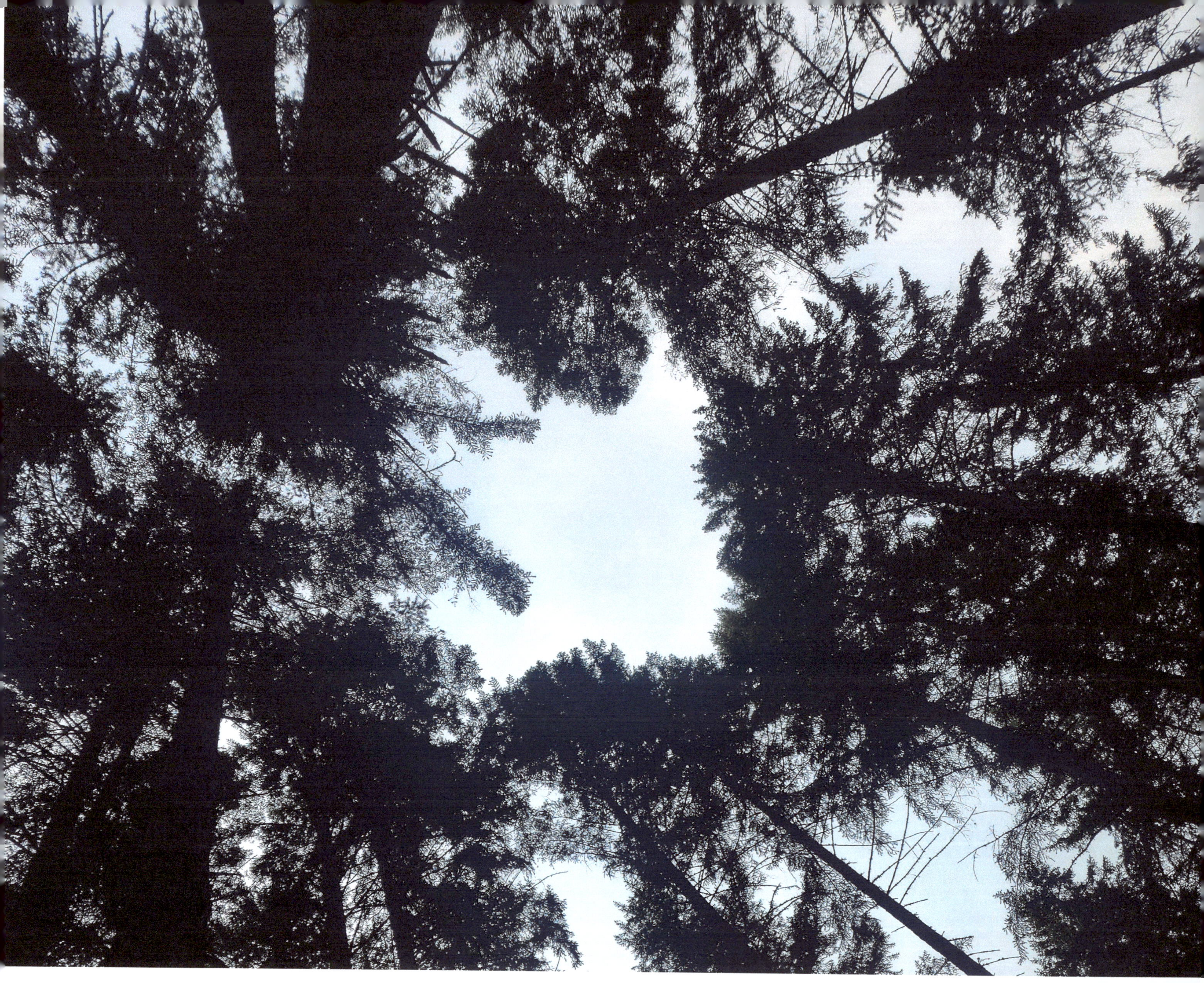

In shadows cast where twilight's whispers fade,
The ghosts of yesteryears in silence roam,
Through halls of time where memories cascade,
They haunt the realms of what was once their home.

A specter's sigh, a fleeting glimpse of light,
They linger in the corners of the mind,
A whisper in the breeze on moonlit night,
A presence felt by those who dare to find.

Are they but echoes of a past now gone,
Or guardians of secrets left untold?
In realms unseen, where shades of dusk are drawn,
They wander through the mysteries of old.

The phantom souls that drift 'twixt dark and gleam,
In spectral realms, you linger, haunt, and dream.

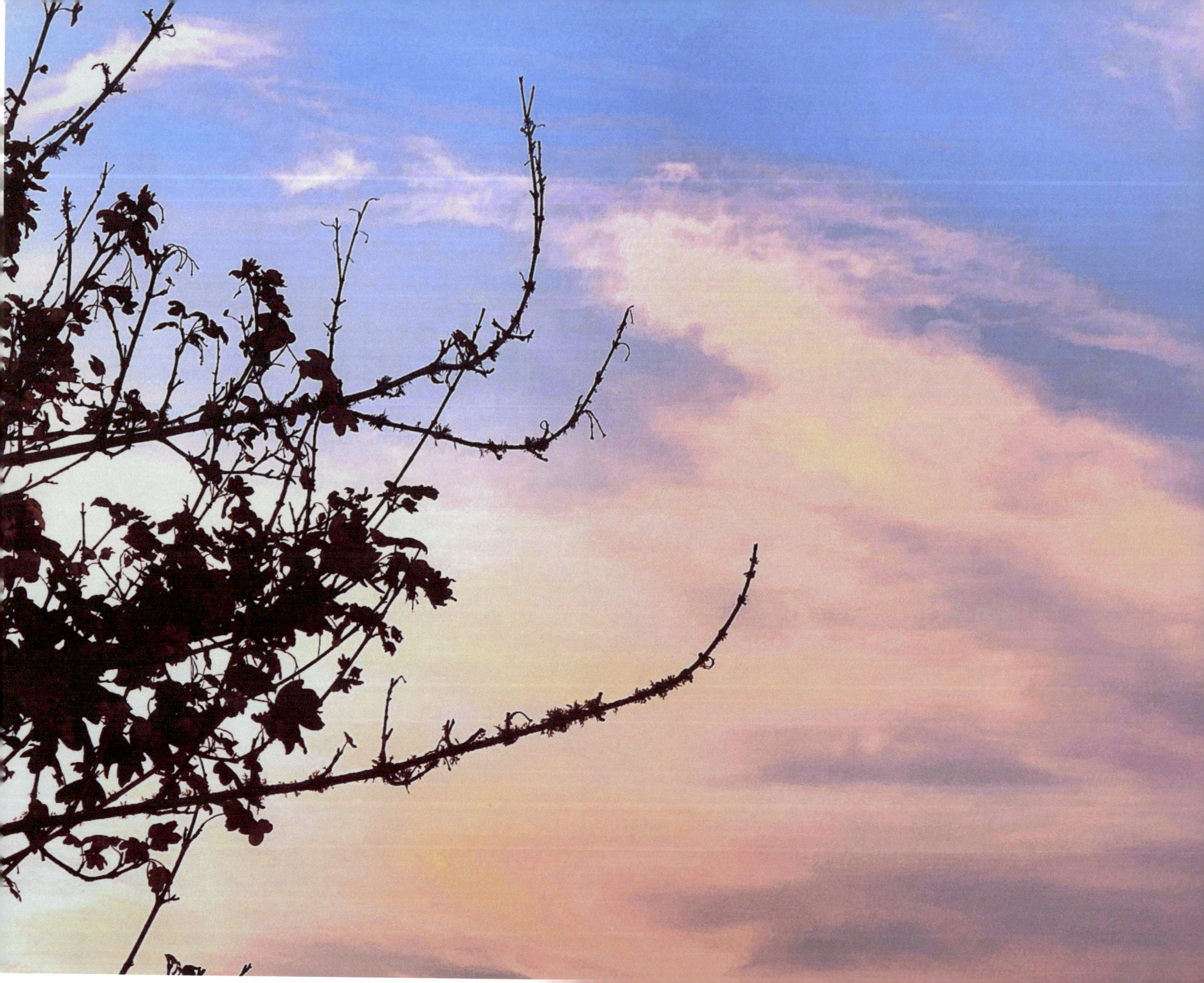

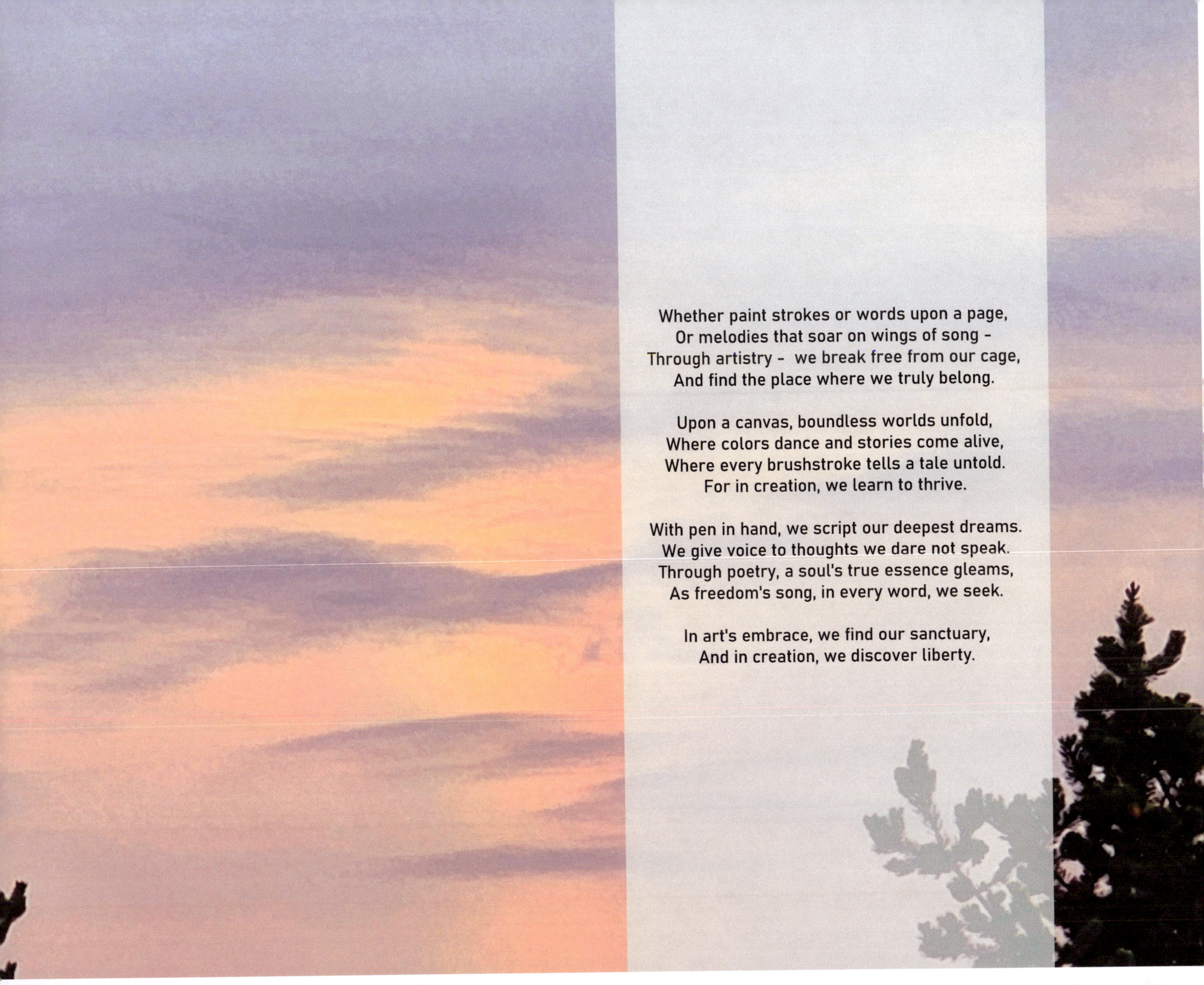

Whether paint strokes or words upon a page,
Or melodies that soar on wings of song –
Through artistry – we break free from our cage,
And find the place where we truly belong.

Upon a canvas, boundless worlds unfold,
Where colors dance and stories come alive,
Where every brushstroke tells a tale untold.
For in creation, we learn to thrive.

With pen in hand, we script our deepest dreams.
We give voice to thoughts we dare not speak.
Through poetry, a soul's true essence gleams,
As freedom's song, in every word, we seek.

In art's embrace, we find our sanctuary,
And in creation, we discover liberty.

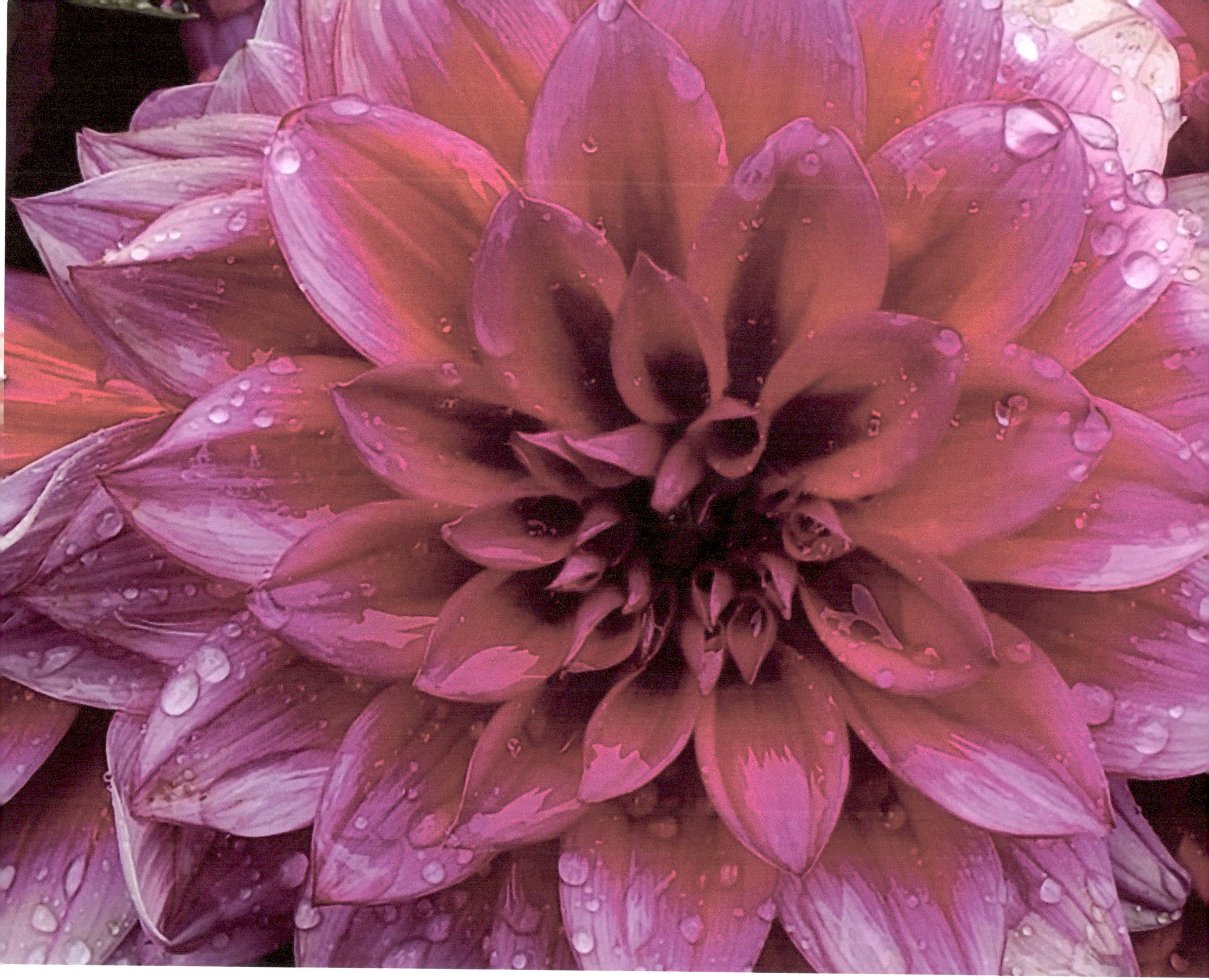

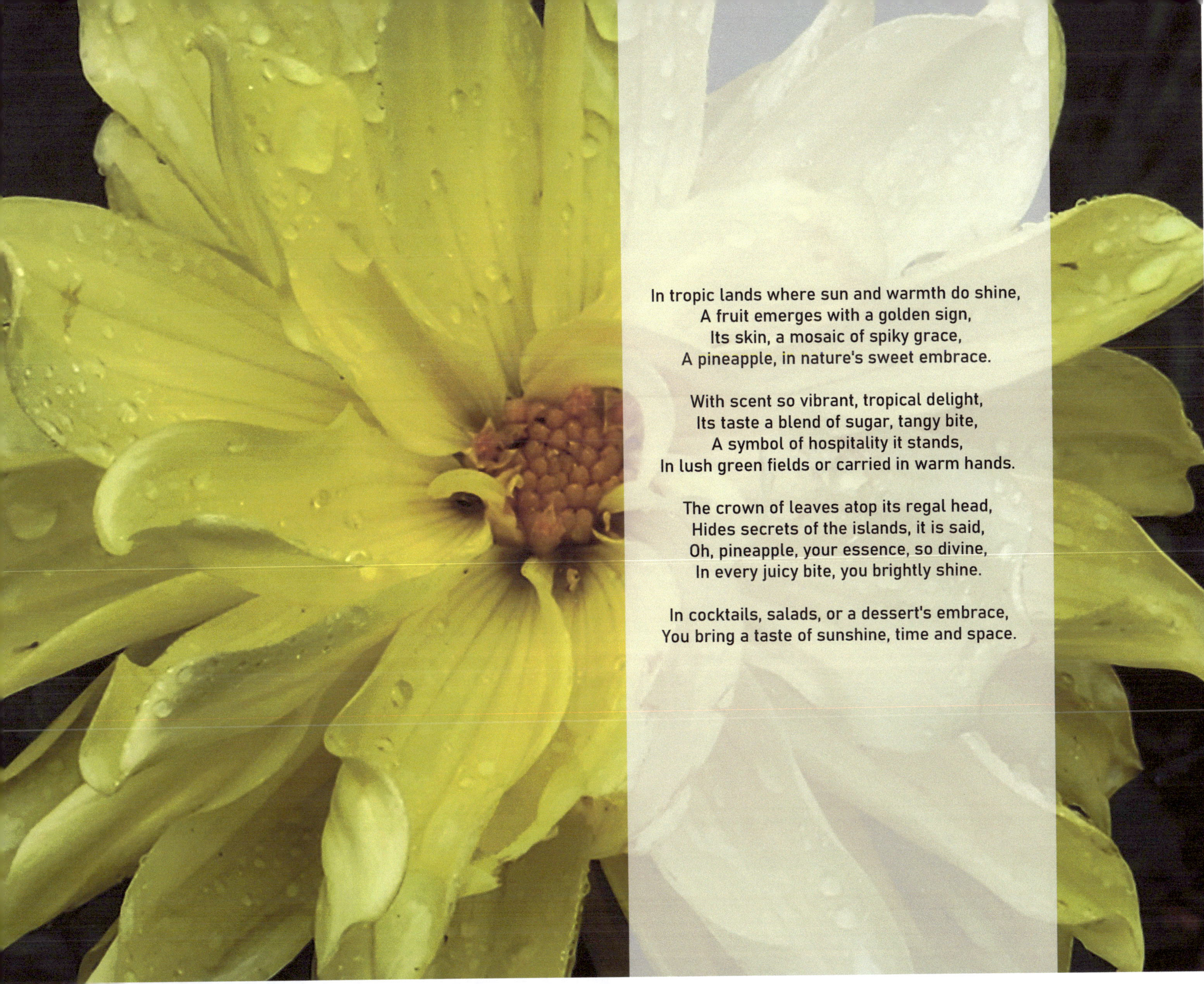

In tropic lands where sun and warmth do shine,
A fruit emerges with a golden sign,
Its skin, a mosaic of spiky grace,
A pineapple, in nature's sweet embrace.

With scent so vibrant, tropical delight,
Its taste a blend of sugar, tangy bite,
A symbol of hospitality it stands,
In lush green fields or carried in warm hands.

The crown of leaves atop its regal head,
Hides secrets of the islands, it is said,
Oh, pineapple, your essence, so divine,
In every juicy bite, you brightly shine.

In cocktails, salads, or a dessert's embrace,
You bring a taste of sunshine, time and space.

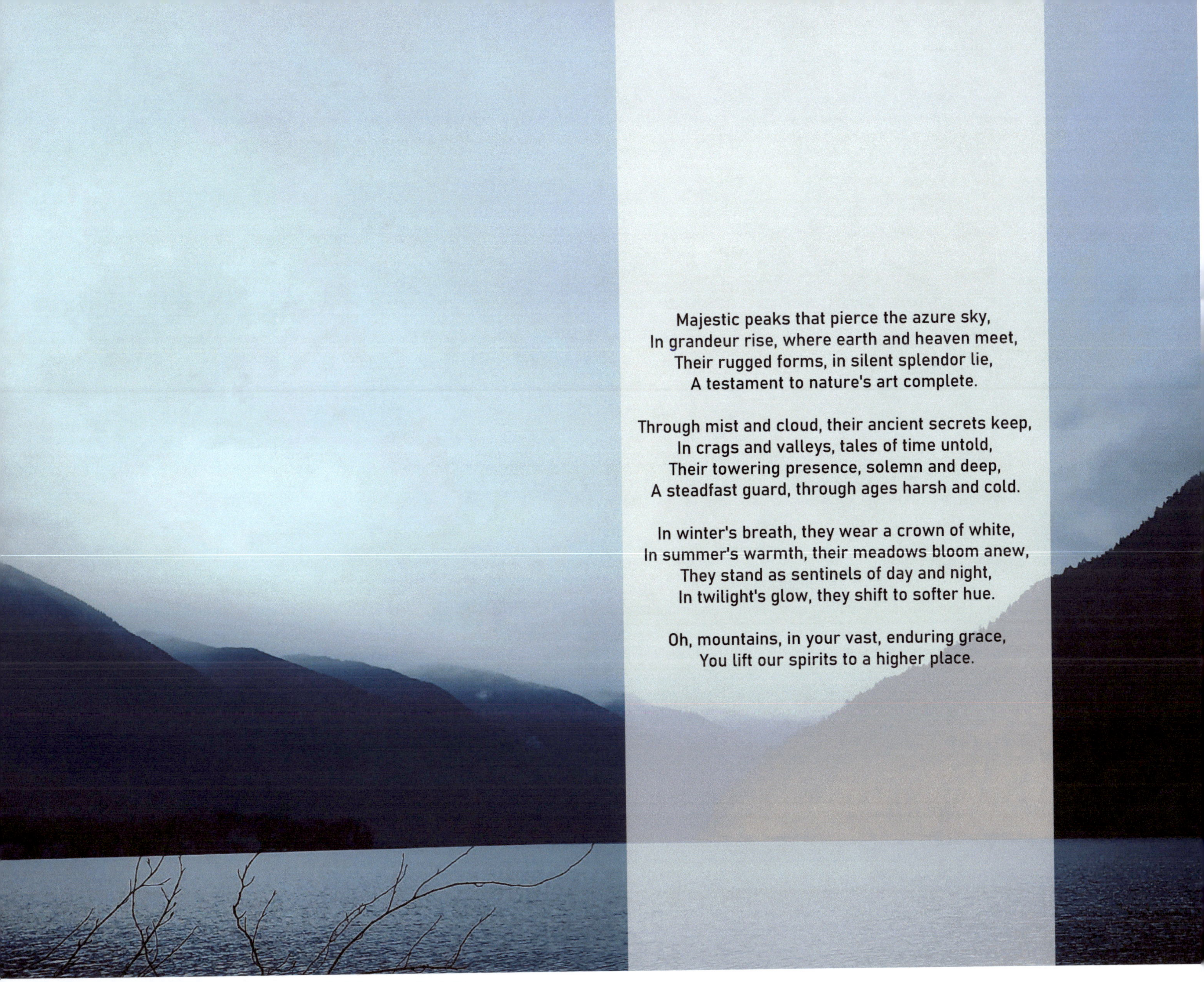

Majestic peaks that pierce the azure sky,
In grandeur rise, where earth and heaven meet,
Their rugged forms, in silent splendor lie,
A testament to nature's art complete.

Through mist and cloud, their ancient secrets keep,
In crags and valleys, tales of time untold,
Their towering presence, solemn and deep,
A steadfast guard, through ages harsh and cold.

In winter's breath, they wear a crown of white,
In summer's warmth, their meadows bloom anew,
They stand as sentinels of day and night,
In twilight's glow, they shift to softer hue.

Oh, mountains, in your vast, enduring grace,
You lift our spirits to a higher place.

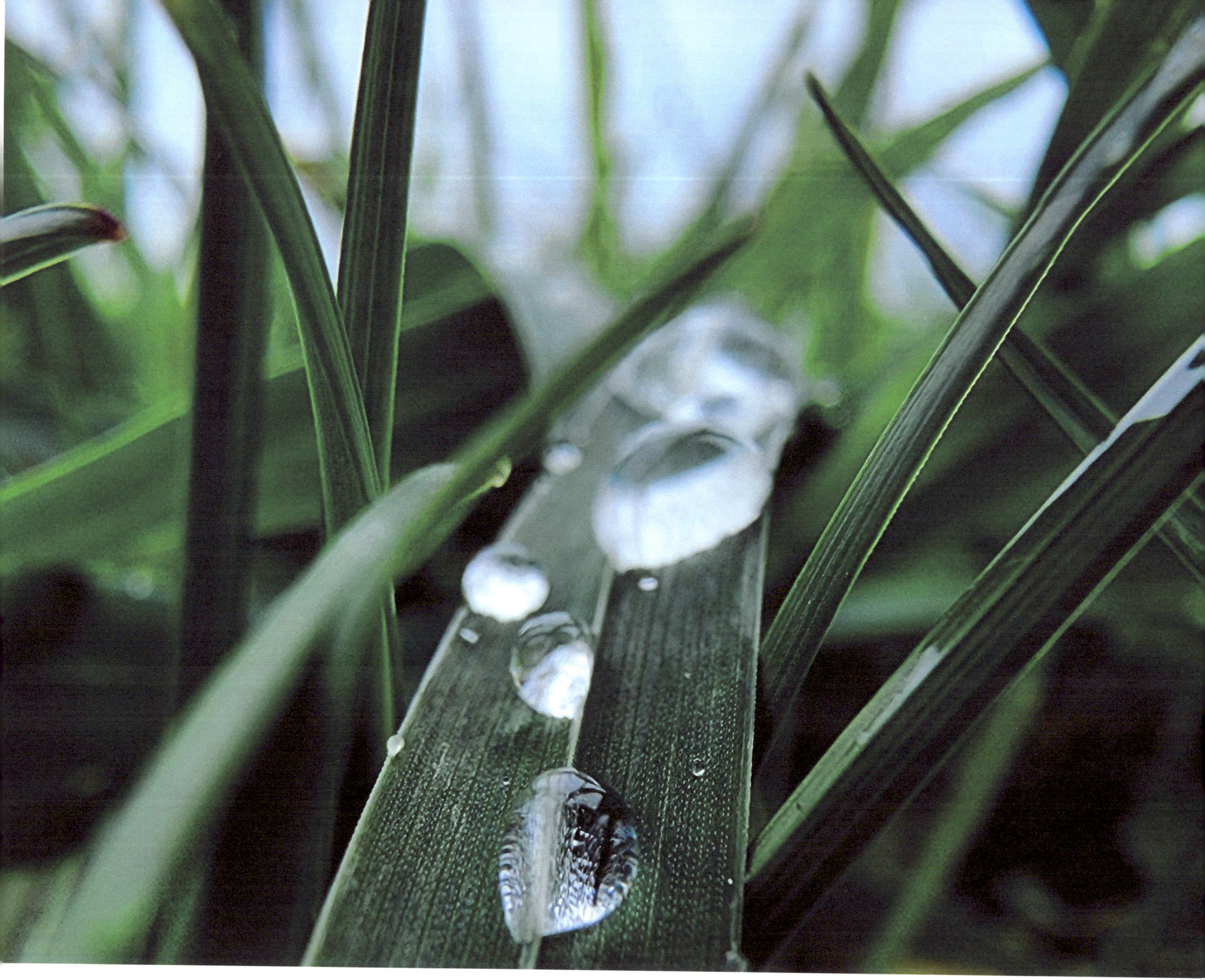

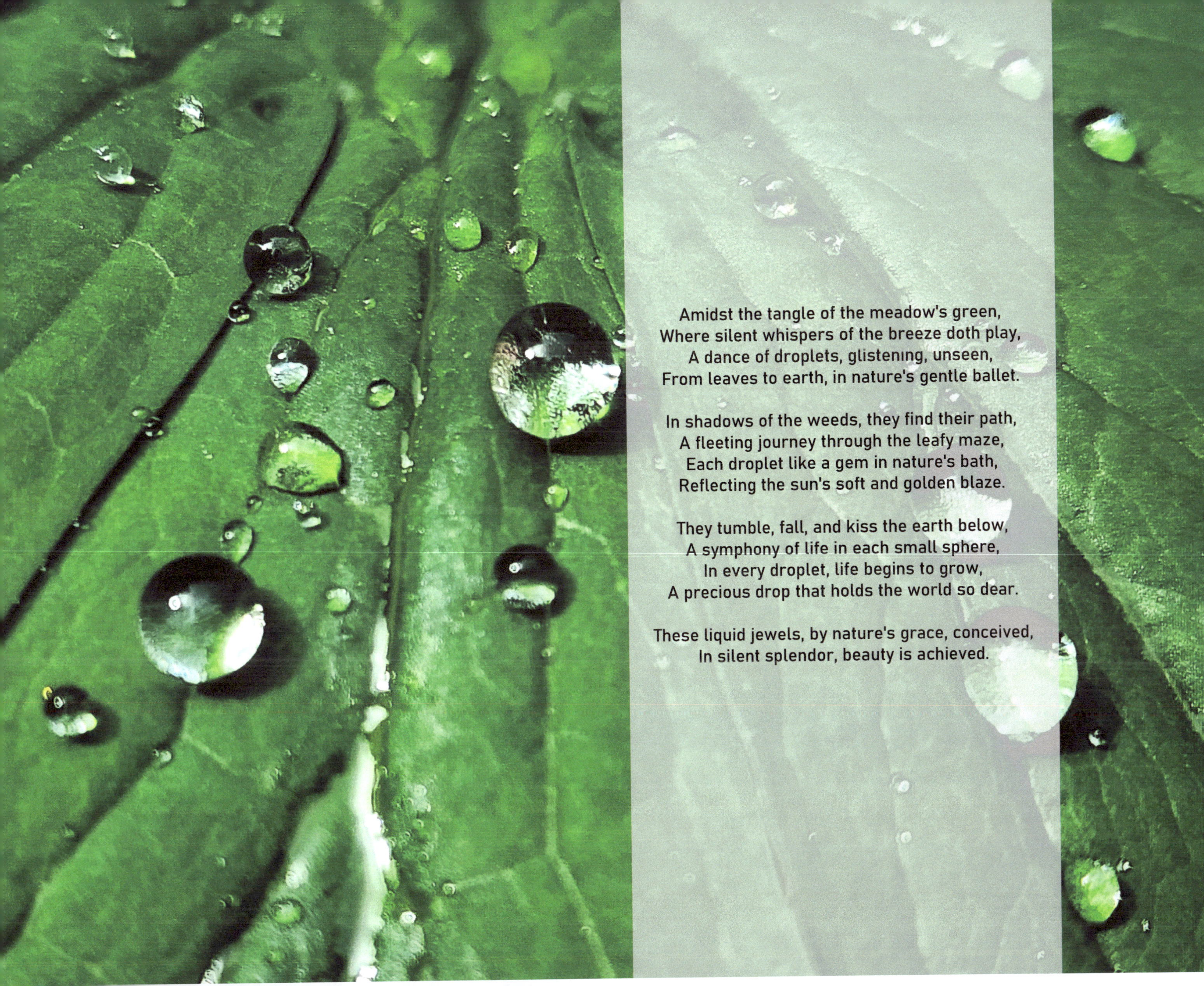

Amidst the tangle of the meadow's green,
Where silent whispers of the breeze doth play,
A dance of droplets, glistening, unseen,
From leaves to earth, in nature's gentle ballet.

In shadows of the weeds, they find their path,
A fleeting journey through the leafy maze,
Each droplet like a gem in nature's bath,
Reflecting the sun's soft and golden blaze.

They tumble, fall, and kiss the earth below,
A symphony of life in each small sphere,
In every droplet, life begins to grow,
A precious drop that holds the world so dear.

These liquid jewels, by nature's grace, conceived,
In silent splendor, beauty is achieved.

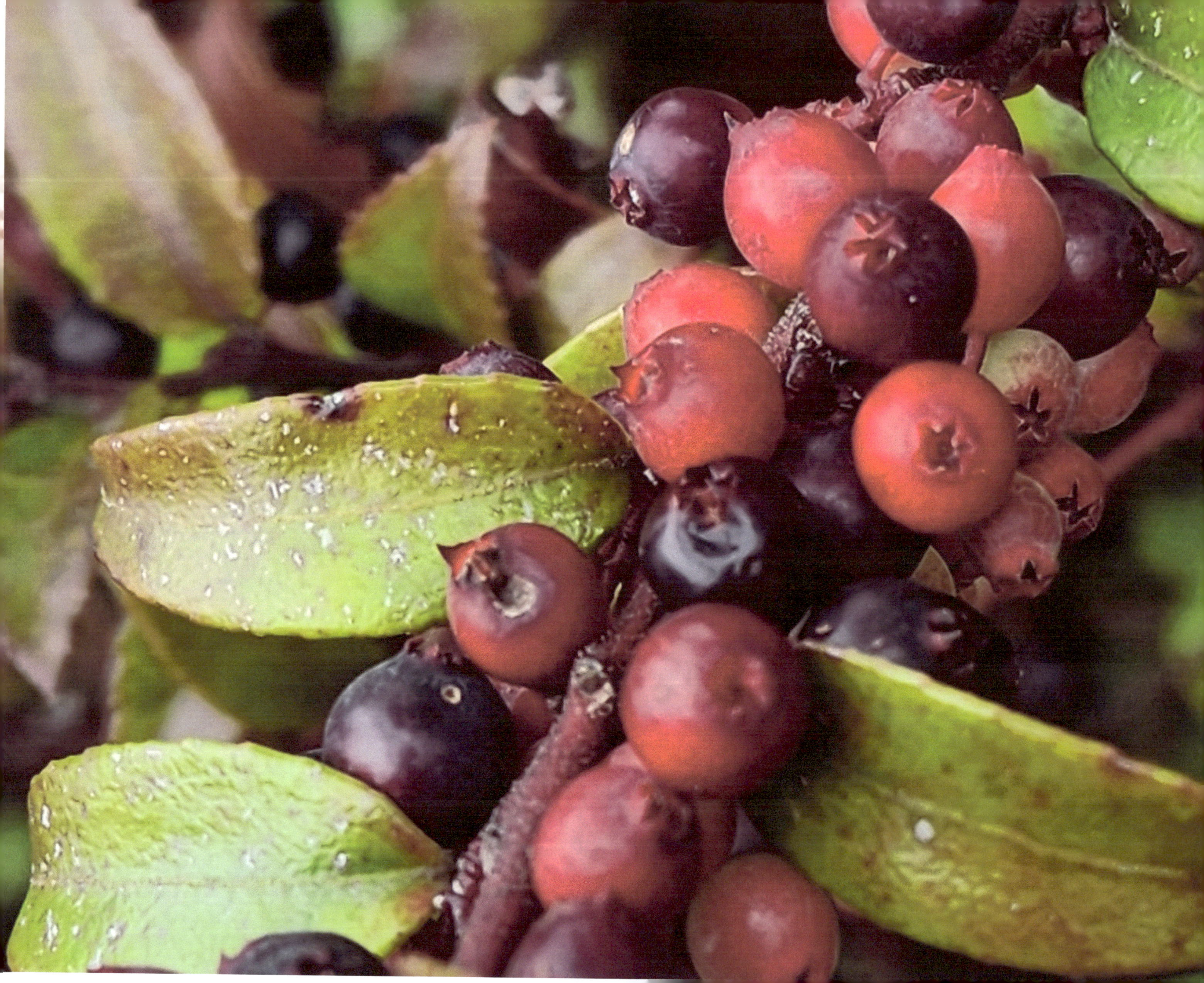

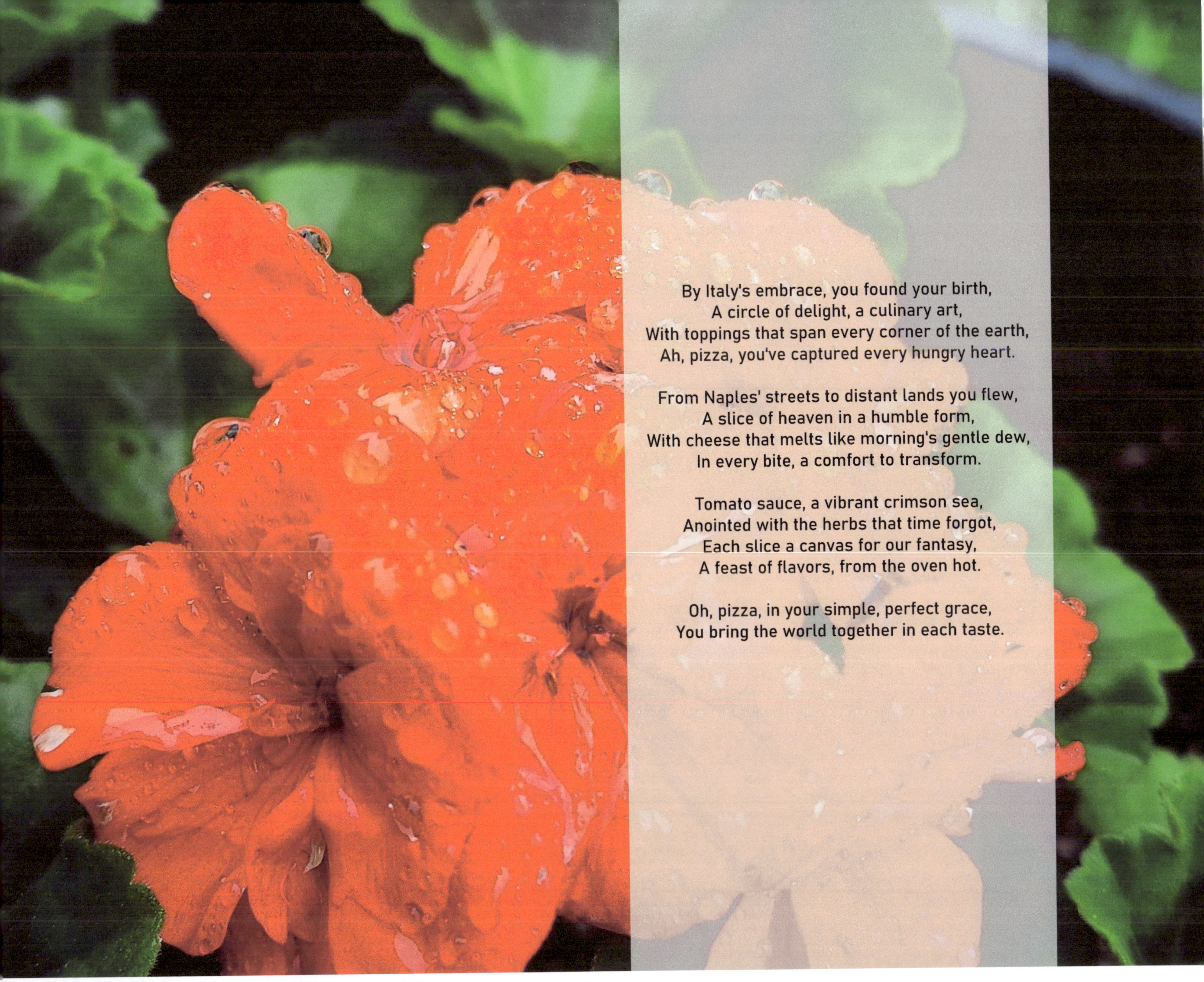

By Italy's embrace, you found your birth,
A circle of delight, a culinary art,
With toppings that span every corner of the earth,
Ah, pizza, you've captured every hungry heart.

From Naples' streets to distant lands you flew,
A slice of heaven in a humble form,
With cheese that melts like morning's gentle dew,
In every bite, a comfort to transform.

Tomato sauce, a vibrant crimson sea,
Anointed with the herbs that time forgot,
Each slice a canvas for our fantasy,
A feast of flavors, from the oven hot.

Oh, pizza, in your simple, perfect grace,
You bring the world together in each taste.

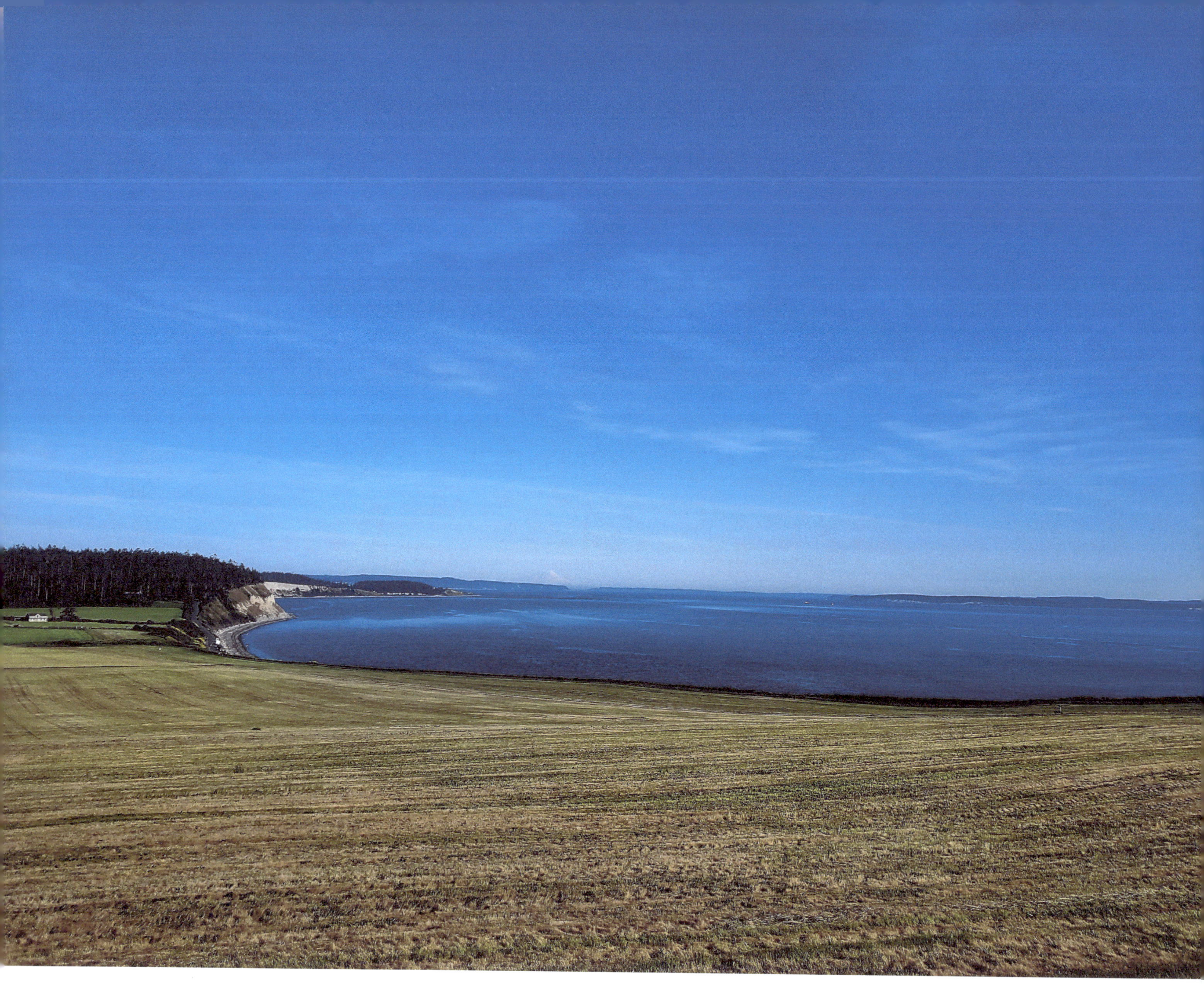

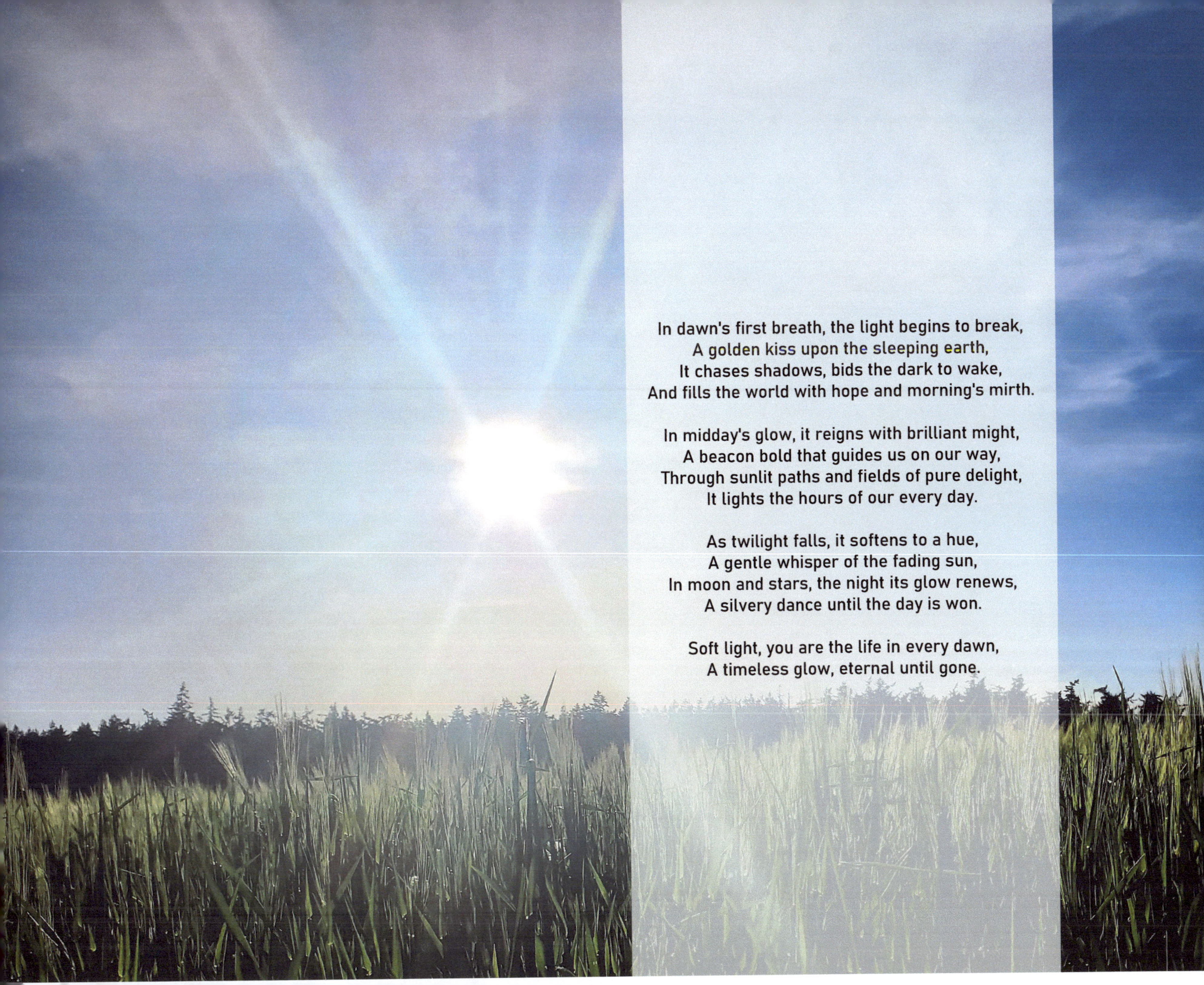

In dawn's first breath, the light begins to break,
A golden kiss upon the sleeping earth,
It chases shadows, bids the dark to wake,
And fills the world with hope and morning's mirth.

In midday's glow, it reigns with brilliant might,
A beacon bold that guides us on our way,
Through sunlit paths and fields of pure delight,
It lights the hours of our every day.

As twilight falls, it softens to a hue,
A gentle whisper of the fading sun,
In moon and stars, the night its glow renews,
A silvery dance until the day is won.

Soft light, you are the life in every dawn,
A timeless glow, eternal until gone.

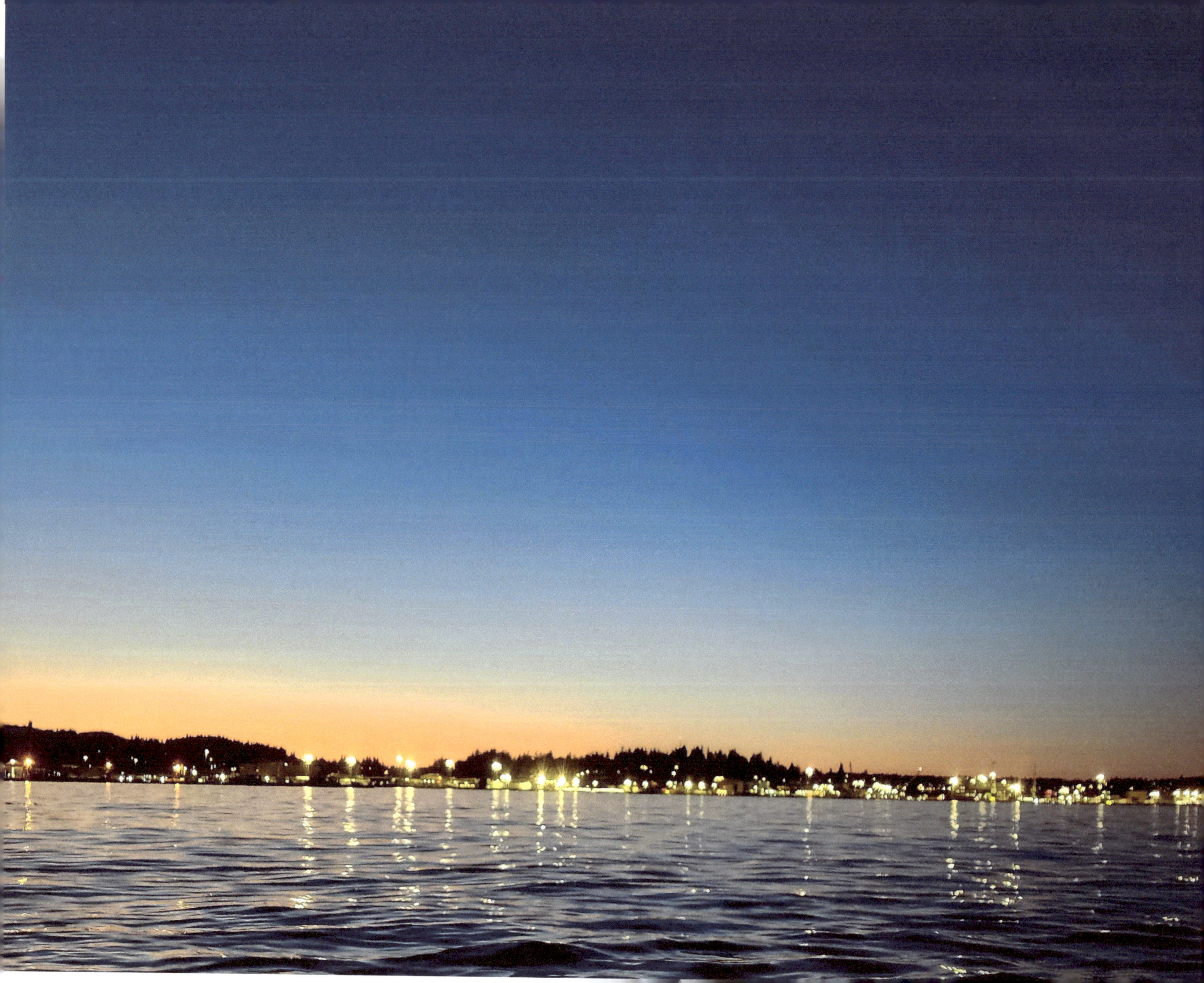

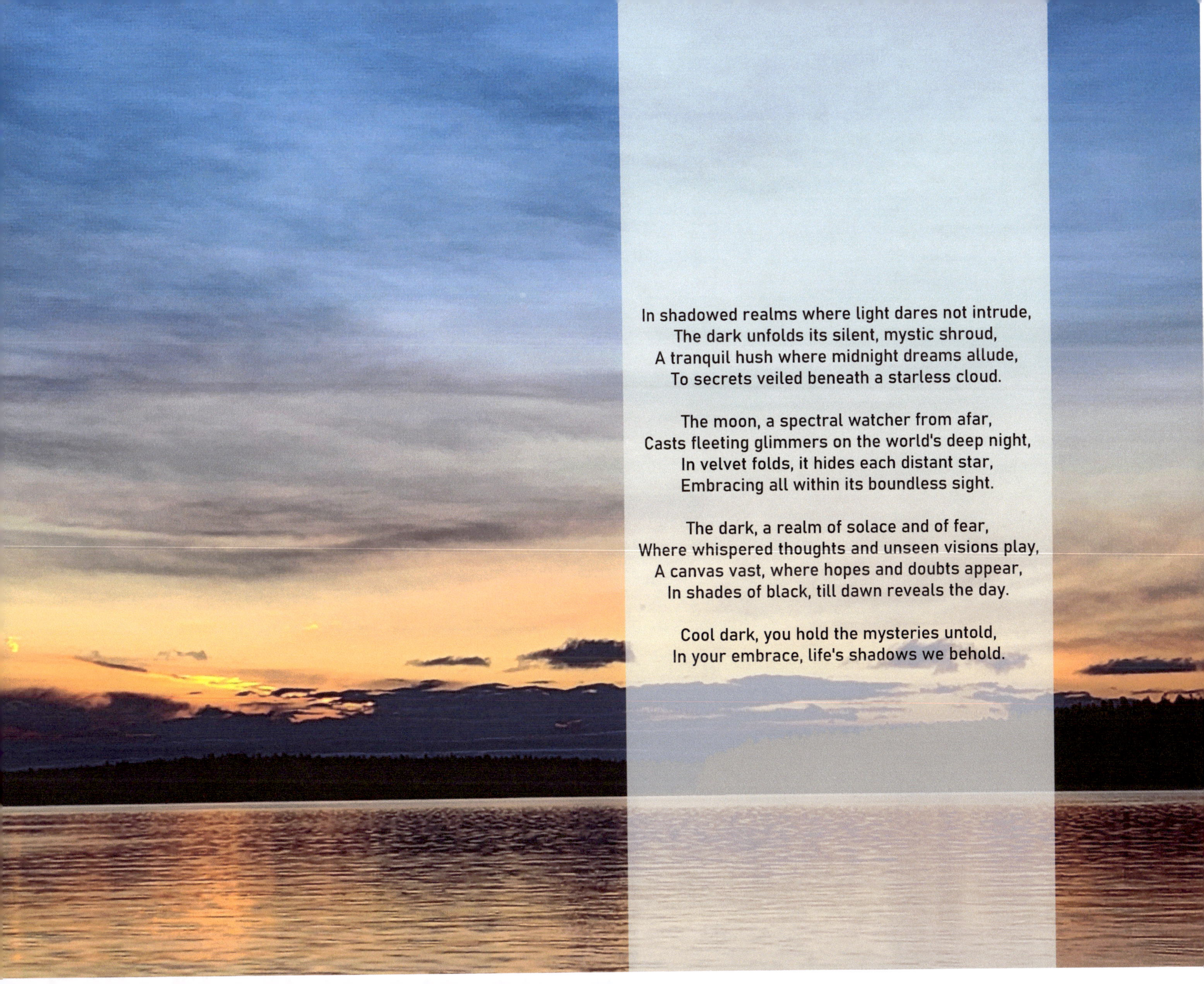

In shadowed realms where light dares not intrude,
The dark unfolds its silent, mystic shroud,
A tranquil hush where midnight dreams allude,
To secrets veiled beneath a starless cloud.

The moon, a spectral watcher from afar,
Casts fleeting glimmers on the world's deep night,
In velvet folds, it hides each distant star,
Embracing all within its boundless sight.

The dark, a realm of solace and of fear,
Where whispered thoughts and unseen visions play,
A canvas vast, where hopes and doubts appear,
In shades of black, till dawn reveals the day.

Cool dark, you hold the mysteries untold,
In your embrace, life's shadows we behold.

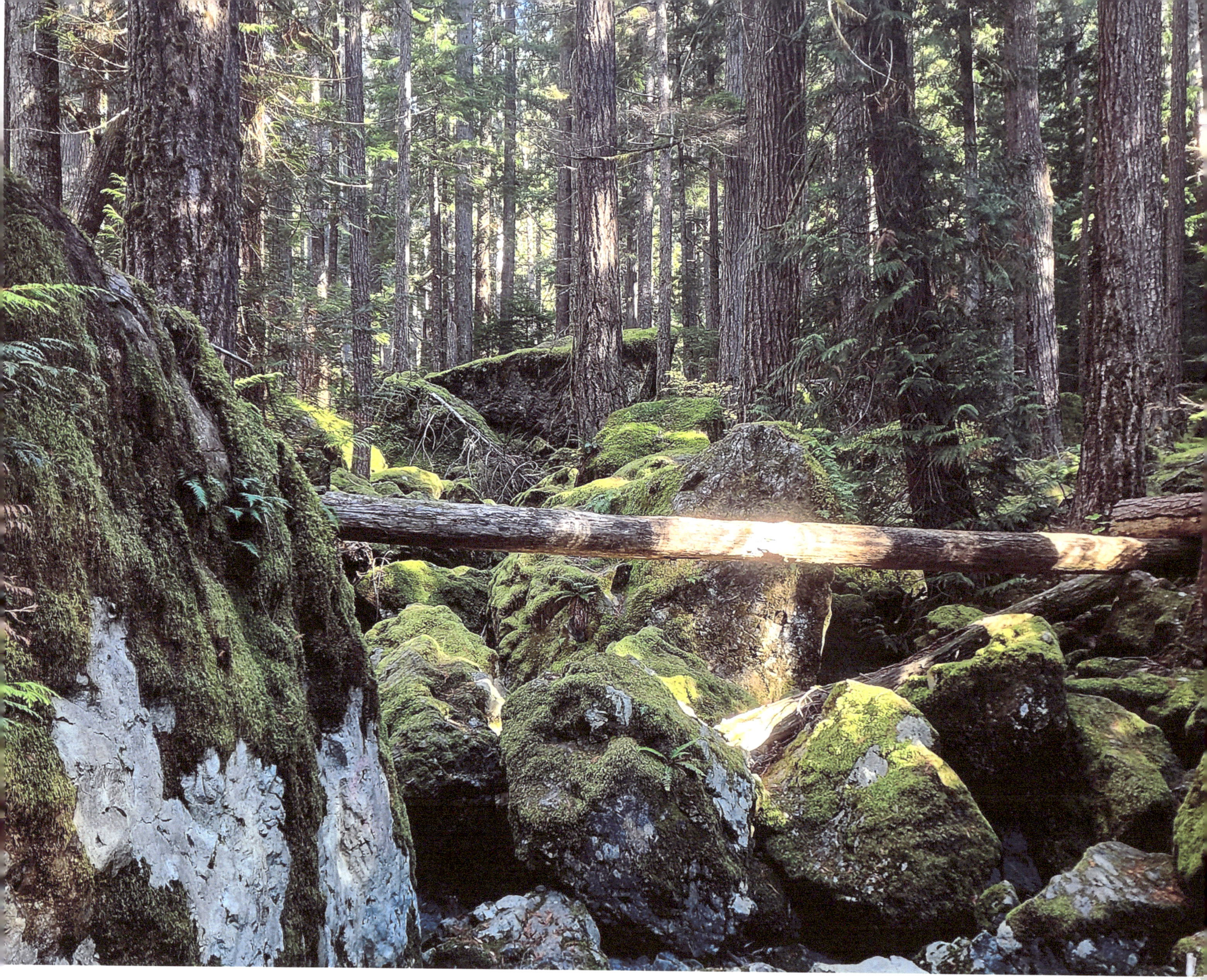

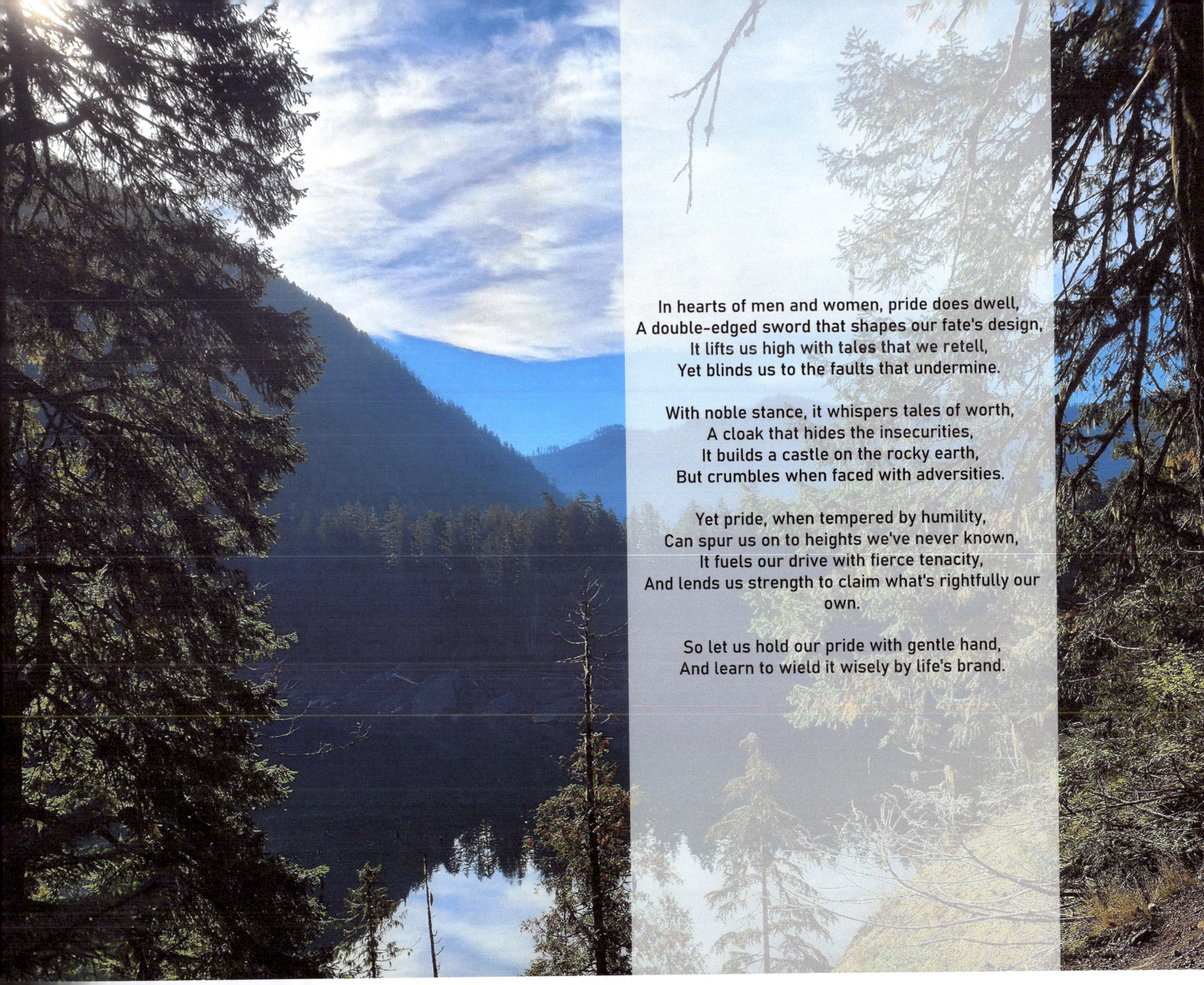

In hearts of men and women, pride does dwell,
A double-edged sword that shapes our fate's design,
It lifts us high with tales that we retell,
Yet blinds us to the faults that undermine.

With noble stance, it whispers tales of worth,
A cloak that hides the insecurities,
It builds a castle on the rocky earth,
But crumbles when faced with adversities.

Yet pride, when tempered by humility,
Can spur us on to heights we've never known,
It fuels our drive with fierce tenacity,
And lends us strength to claim what's rightfully our own.

So let us hold our pride with gentle hand,
And learn to wield it wisely by life's brand.

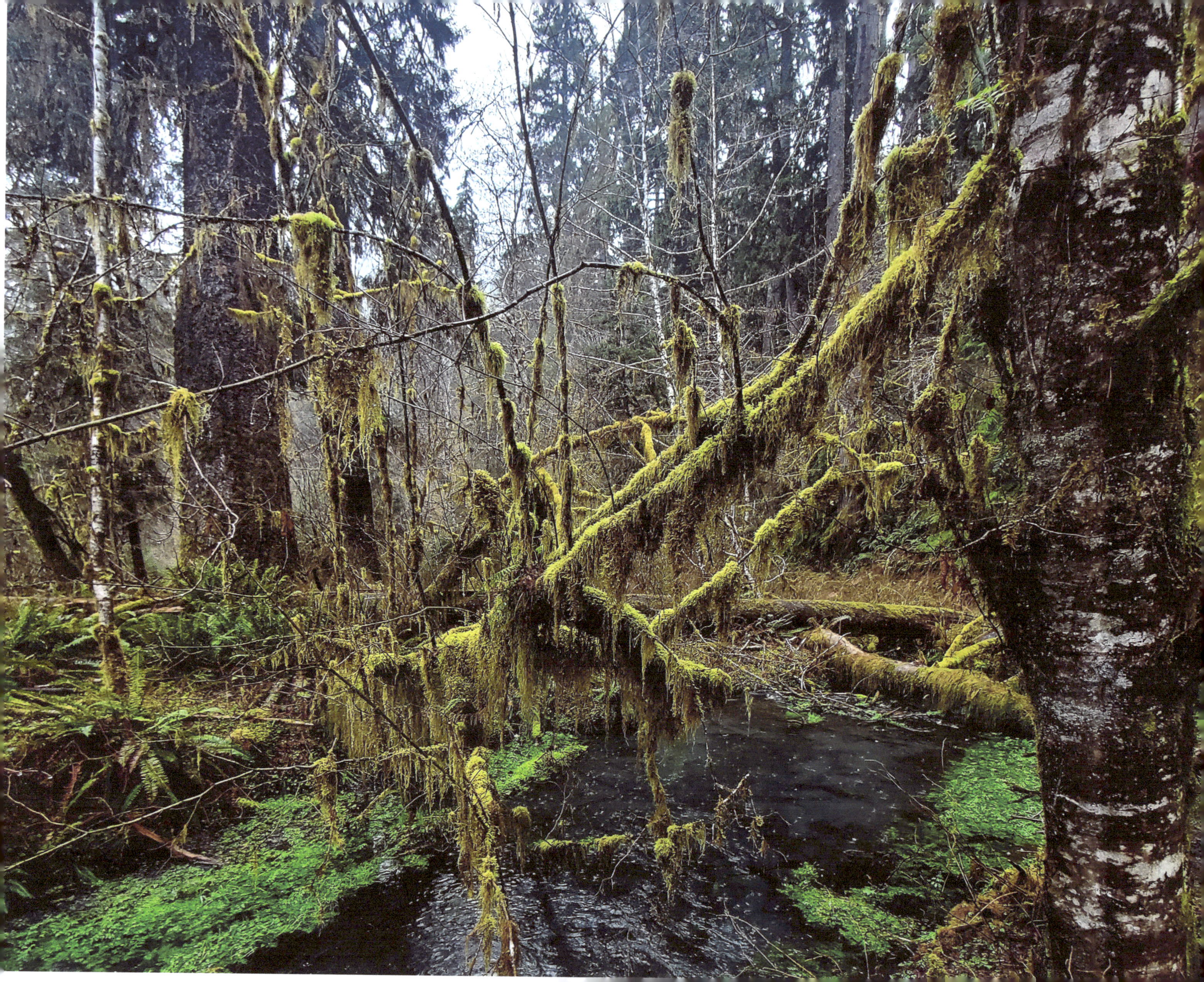

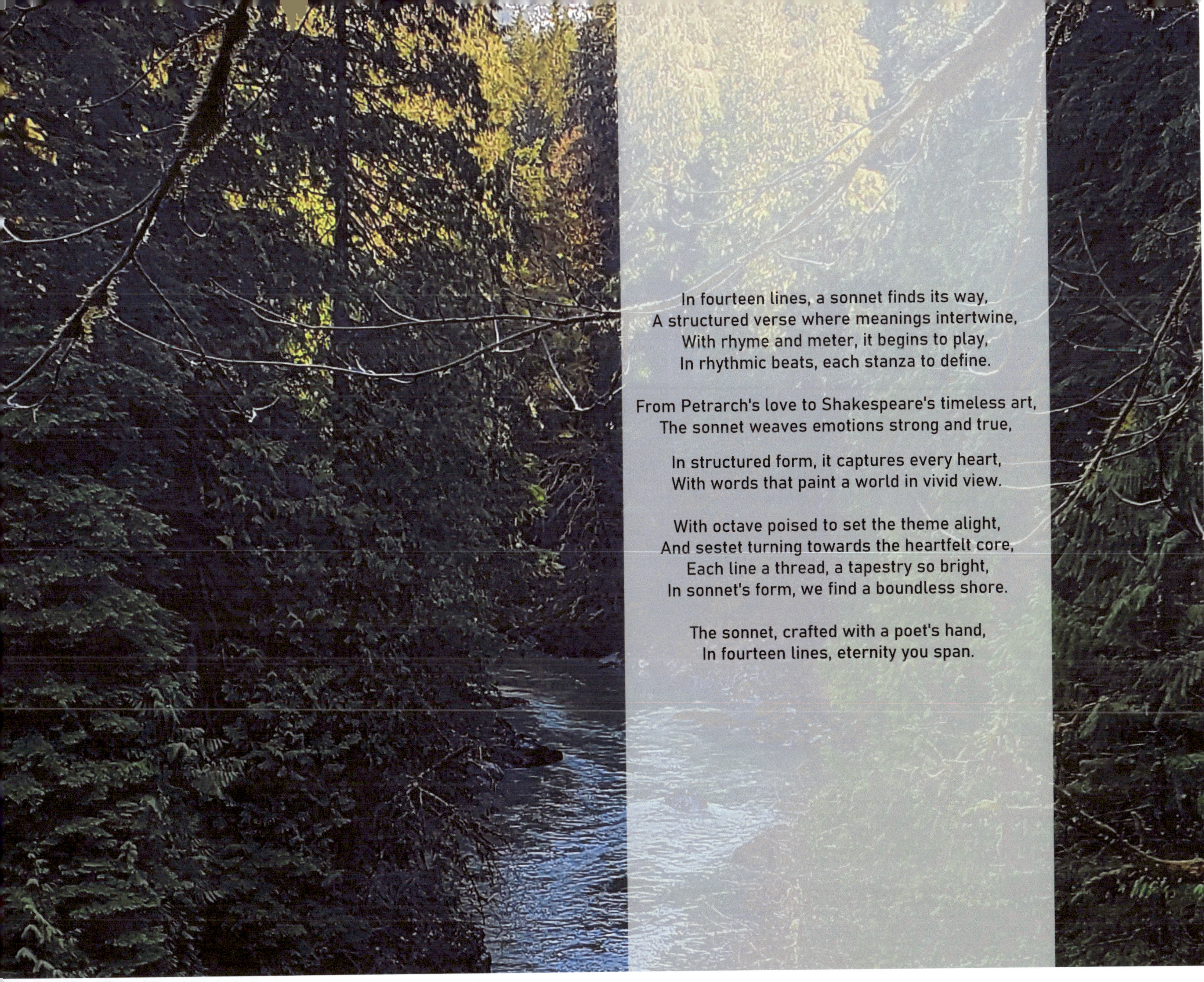

In fourteen lines, a sonnet finds its way,
A structured verse where meanings intertwine,
With rhyme and meter, it begins to play,
In rhythmic beats, each stanza to define.

From Petrarch's love to Shakespeare's timeless art,
The sonnet weaves emotions strong and true,

In structured form, it captures every heart,
With words that paint a world in vivid view.

With octave poised to set the theme alight,
And sestet turning towards the heartfelt core,
Each line a thread, a tapestry so bright,
In sonnet's form, we find a boundless shore.

The sonnet, crafted with a poet's hand,
In fourteen lines, eternity you span.

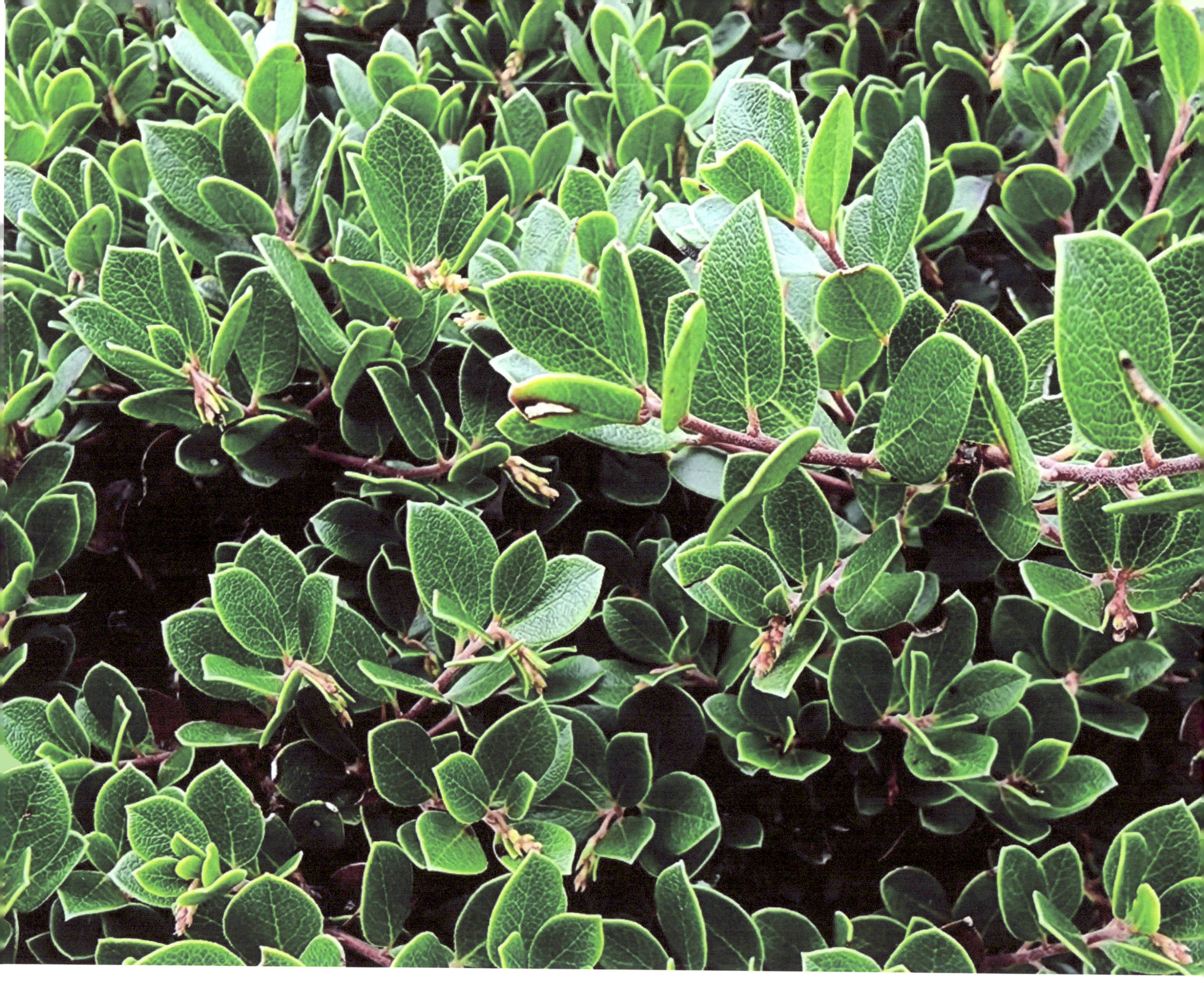

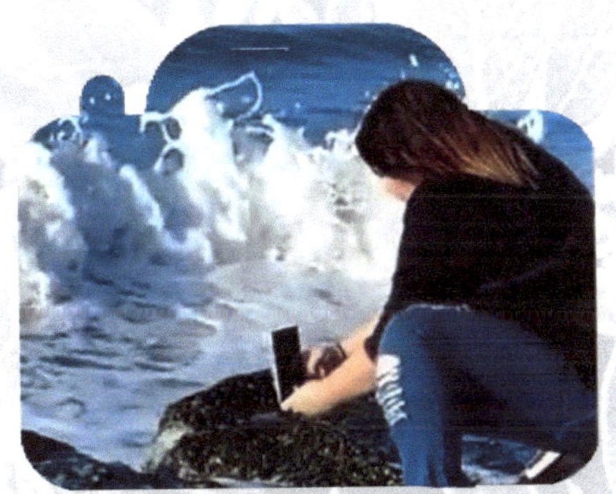

Sharron is the co-founder of Arledge Comics and founder of Sharrone & Only Photography. She's been in the publishing game for eight years and pursuing photography for half that time. She finds nature very grounding, and photography as a way to capture the beauty between the hustle and bustle of busy everyday life. She says: "Our lives are surrounded by natural wonders, but so few are able to slow down and actually see how epic our home really is."

Jordaan is a comic writer and founder of Arledge Comics. While they've been in the comic industry for nearly a decade, their first forays into writing were actually poetic in nature. They consider themselves a cotemporary sonneteer, writing about literally anything and everything in the form and style that some English professors have called "just as ugly now as it was then." (You know who you are, and I'm still writing wing'd.)

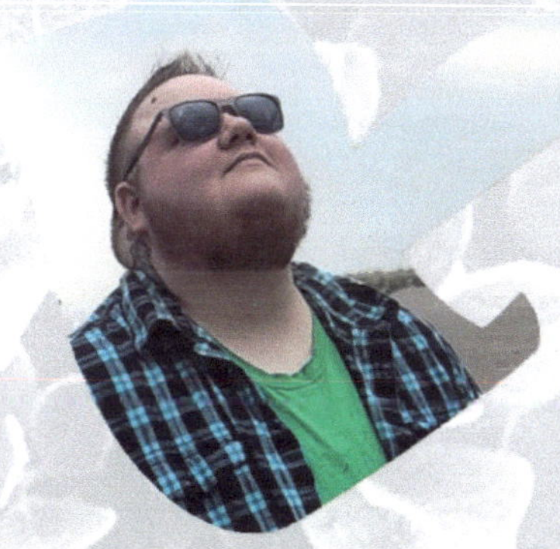